Ranger Heart:

A Naturalist Learns How to Love After Loss

B.A. Woodland

_____

Ranger Heart:

A Naturalist Learns How to Love
After Loss

Vanguard Press

VANGUARD PAPERBACK

© Copyright 2023
B.A. Woodland

The right of B.A. Woodland to be identified as author of this work has been asserted by her in accordance with the Copyright, Designs and Patents Act 1988.

All Rights Reserved

No reproduction, copy or transmission of this publication may be made without written permission.
No paragraph of this publication may be reproduced, copied or transmitted save with the written permission of the publisher, or in accordance with the provisions of the Copyright Act 1956 (as amended).

Any person who commits any unauthorised act in relation to this publication may be liable to criminal prosecution and civil claims for damages.

A CIP catalogue record for this title is available from the British Library.

ISBN 978 1 80016 897 8

*Vanguard Press is an imprint of
Pegasus Elliot Mackenzie Publishers Ltd.*
www.pegasuspublishers.com

First Published in 2023

**Vanguard Press
Sheraton House Castle Park
Cambridge England**

Printed & Bound in Great Britain

For all of my loved ones and relations, especially my dear strong mother, who encouraged me to have ambitions beyond all boundaries and follow my passion.

Introduction

I dreamt of attending Prescott College in Arizona after high school. When I read the course catalog explaining the field natural history classes and wilderness component, I felt something resonate deep within. Not only did the description seem to capture what I wanted in higher education, it tugged at some bound-up part of me that made me think that if I attended Prescott, I could untangle myself and follow the thread of my life to a place that finally felt like *mine*. After sharing a house with eleven siblings, I was eager to strike out on my own.

Ultimately, I did not attend Prescott. My life trajectory could have been completely different had I applied and been accepted there. Or, it could have been quite similar to how my life unfolded. I will never know. What I do know, however, is that there has been a consistent throughline in my story, which is that I always wanted to be as intimately in communion with nature and wilderness as my work and life would allow. Therefore, I knew I wanted a job that would enable me to live in wild spaces, and I wanted a partner who could match my enthusiasm for the outdoors but would not eclipse my goals with his own ambitions. What I had to learn over time was that my particular hungers could only be fed by consuming the right balance of wilderness, community, and love. Too much wilderness without the other two and I would sink into loneliness. Too much time spent investing in relationships and I would lose sight of myself. Too much dependency on romance and I would begin to feel isolated.

I have not found the secret to managing consistent levels of all three, since the variables within a life inevitably throw us off balance. What I do know is that in this life, my aim is to consistently move in the direction of that balance. It is the ever-shifting goal post. I have set my sights on it, but I know that it will mostly stay out of reach. The trick is to notice those magnificent moments when I feel perfectly in alignment, and to feel gratitude—even if only briefly—when I feel wholly nourished by wilderness, community, and love. Because to attain these perfect, peaceful, fleeting moments of joy is the stuff of life. I have found that my personal recipe consists of wilderness, community, and love, but it is up to each individual person to discover the unique blend that makes them feel whole. This little book is my humble attempt at relaying experiences and stories from my time as a park ranger and naturalist that have helped shape the person I have become: someone who seeks joy by finding the miracle in each acorn, in each conversation with a dear friend, in each kiss from the person I love. Each of the following stories tells a larger story: one of a woman who has devoted herself to joy. This is not a tale of a trail of lost loves, but rather one of found experiences and shared adventures. Call this book a devotional, a love story, or a collection of essays—it is my gift of joy to you. Though I did not attend Prescott College, I did earn a degree in the natural sciences from State University of New York (SUNY) at Cortland, and steadily worked toward my goal of applying and being accepted to work for the National Park Service. My work and whims took me from my home in Upstate New York to Washington D.C., from the deserts of Zion and the Grand Canyon to the tundra and seas of Alaska, from the gaping valley of Yosemite to my current home in Colorado. Throughout my career, I have fought wildfires, hiked well over ten thousand miles, paddled through crocodile-infested waters, and have been charged by grizzlies. In the end, I did just fine for an East Coast girl striving to carve out a life of her own making after leaving the nest.

If you are inclined towards a career in the environment and sciences—especially if you are a woman—the National Parks Service is a good place to hang your hat. Women need stories of other strong women. Though my mother was a homebody, she has always been the strongest female role model in my life. She modeled grit, resilience, and unconditional love. She was not fighting fires or scaring off grizzlies, but she raised a dozen children mostly on her own and handled just about every situation that came her way with humility and an open heart.

The original people of my homeland in the northeastern United States are the Haudenosaunee, 'People of the Longhouse', or the Onondaga Nation. In sharing the story of my roots, I want to honor the place where my life began. I grew up learning about the Onondaga Nation, part of the Iroquois Tribe of Six Nations—Onondaga, Seneca, Cayuga, Oneida, Mohawk, and Tuscarora—and how it is one of the only known democratic, matriarchal societies. Women were reportedly allowed into tribal meetings and were listened to and respected, often serving as deciding members of the tribe, helping to make important decisions for the benefit of the entire community. This book is for the people whose ancestral land I grew up on. It is for women who want to work in the wilderness. Most of all, it is for any woman who wants to write her own story.

To women and girls around the world: YOU are a park ranger. YOU are a wildlife manager, a researcher, wilderness ranger, a wildland firefighter, a trail crew leader, a heavy machinery operator, an interpreter, and a superintendent. YOU are a rock climber, a mountaineer, an outdoors person, a backpacker, a ski mountaineer, and an adventurer. The wilderness belongs to you. The story of America's public lands will be written by you and about YOU. What will your story be?

We all have to go out into the world to find our own way. The stories that follow describe the path I took. I would sincerely love to hear about where your path takes you.

Part 1
Advice for Women with Grit

1
Be a Life, not a Number

My mother gave birth to and raised twelve children.

"What number are you?" people often ask me, which feels diminishing to a woman who wants to stand out.

I am number nine, with seven brothers and four sisters. Together we span an age range of eighteen years. At times, growing up, I felt invisible. On the rare occasion that our fourteen-person household went out in public together, it was a spectacle. At church, we would take up an entire pew. I became just a number, wedged in between the others in the total count.

When I think of my mother, I think of her hands, because they were always holding something—dishes, garden tools, clothing, children. Since my mother always had her hands full, my siblings and I tried to help where we could. While she was at work, my mother would phone home and ask me to put a pot of water on the stove.

"Pour in two pounds of dried pasta," she instructed. "We're going to make macaroni and cheese."

My siblings and I were the helpers, but she was the matriarch, the fearless leader of our home. She'd had to be, because my father died when I was six, leaving our family without a household income, my siblings and I without a father, and my mother without the love of her life. She dug deep so the rest of us wouldn't have to.

"Your mother is a saint," people would say when they learned of her resilience. They were spellbound, astonished that she kept such a tidy house and that all her children were well looked after. They were curious for answers.

"All you need is soap and water," my mother would say.

Our house was a continuous chaotic carnival. Seemingly mile-high stacks of dishes teetered and mountains of laundry towered. The scent of laundry detergent hung in the air. Piles of athletic gear from just about every sport were laid out in many corners. Bedrooms were furnished with bunkbeds, one of the rooms crammed with two sets.

Each time my mother got pregnant, she did her best to hide it, afraid what members of the community might say. After all, twelve of us were born, she would joke, "I only had sex twelve times." But when I looked at my mother, I didn't see a woman who was an easy target for gossip; I saw someone who had grit—someone who could thrive during these pregnancies, run a household, and raise a dozen children in a loving environment.

My mother practiced an easygoing parenting style, almost bordering on laissez-faire. This meant my siblings and I had a hand in raising one another. But despite my mother's challenges tending to the multitude of needs of each of her children, her love was steady and kind. She never played favorites even when opportunities for favoritism arose. She treated us equally, with respect and dignity. Rarely did she raise her voice or swear. Since these instances were so few and far between, we were mortified and frightened when they did occur.

"Oh hell," she shouted after dropping something heavy on her toe. "Damn it," she cursed after a near miss fender bender.

Because we knew she was already carrying so much, we did not want to add any more weight to her load. We went out of our way to avoid disappointing her. Ultimately, though, there was nothing any of us could do to satisfy the tug my mother felt to expand her identity outside motherhood.

One day, while sitting at the dining room table with a mug of Lipton tea cupped in her hand, my mother confessed, "My brain feels numb from playing so many children's board games and talking to kids all day."

When it was time for my youngest sibling, Christine, to start kindergarten, my mother went back to school to earn a business degree. Up until then, my mother's older brother had been helping to pay the mortgage on our house. I think she had wanted to relieve him of that burden by finding herself a job, but more than that, I think she simply yearned for a life outside the home. Despite the enormous, important role she filled being a single parent to twelve children, she showed us that a woman could desire more for herself than martyrdom and motherhood. She showed us it was okay to want more—to *be* more.

My mother graduated from business school, and she began working full time at the Dale Carnegie Institute. To us, she described her job as 'teaching people how to win friends and influence people'.

After my mother began working, I observed a noticeable shift in her energy when she came home each day. She seemed lighter—*brighter*, somehow—her brain buzzing with intellectual stimulation she could not find among her children. Even though she loved us, her true self had been stifled in that house. I paid close attention to this, certain she was teaching me something, though I did not yet know what.

Eventually, I graduated from high school and moved out of that house—that green, shingled house in Syracuse, New York. That *loud* house. It is the loudness I remember most, and once I left the noise and the crowded space, I sought the quiet and solitude of wilderness. While I loved my family with my whole heart, I loved myself, too. It is only now that I realize that's what my mom had been teaching me—that it's possible to love the people in our lives with our whole heart, and to love ourselves just as much. That doing such a thing isn't a selfish act—it's a *necessary* one. If there's ever an imbalance, a heart can harden. I was seeking to soften my heart, until it was as plush and downy as the head of a cattail, as expansive as the Pacific Ocean, as clear and crystalline as the Little Colorado River. Though I would never raise as many children as my mother had, I was still following in her footsteps, along the well-worn path she had carved, which led—for me—straight from our house into the heart of the wilderness. I longed to trade my cramped quarters and mountains of laundry for open spaces and mountains of evergreens. It was there that I thought I might find a way in which my life was not just measured as a number, and where I could create a life that was entirely my own. I no longer wanted to compete for a seat at the table. I simply wanted to have my *own* table—preferably a picnic table at a campground.

2
Be Like Fire and Make Your Own Weather

I tucked my application inside the manila envelope, kissed it, and sent it off in the mail. Not long after, I was hired for my first paid park service job as a firefighter at Crater Lake National Park.

Though I was a naturalist and biologist hoping to be assigned a position within my skillset, I was grateful for the opportunity to be placed in the National Park Service at all. While I wanted to teach park visitors about the bright-bellied Mazama newt, which is found only at Crater Lake, or to explain the unique ecology of the crater, rimmed with high-elevation whitebark pine and mountain hemlock, I hoped a firefighter position would later lead to an educational position.

I told my mother that I would officially work for the U.S. Department of the Interior as a National Park Service ranger, a dream I'd had for two years, since my junior year of college. She beamed with pride.

I was issued flame-resistant Nomex clothing, a shovel, and a Pulaski—a hand tool that combines an ax and adze in one head. I studied fire behavior and safety and attempted to bond with the men in my crew. Approaching midseason, while many in the crew got sent out on nine large 'project fires' in Oregon, I stayed behind in Crater Lake, fighting smaller fires within the park. Between flare-ups, we did odd jobs in the fire cache, sharpened tools, stayed in shape, and played hacky sack in our down time.

Life as a firefighter was simple, but grueling. Our crew worked tirelessly over a record-breaking fire year. We dug fire lines, long ditches two to three inches deep and six to eight inches wide. We hacked at the ground with our shovels and Pulaskis, digging below the roots. The aim was to use these lines as boundaries to prevent ground fires from surging out of control across the landscape, but fires have behaviors of their own. They can create their own weather and their own wind. They can jump and run; they can rage across entire hillsides in an updraft, flames licking the landscape clean. They can raze entire forests, leveling scrub oak, ponderosa pine, and sagebrush, leaving behind only ash, dust, and the skeletons of scorched trees. For a time, the barren landscape is an affront to the eye, reminiscent of a singed warzone. Eventually, the undergrowth becomes a blaze of color—bright greens and swaths of pink from fireweed blossoms. What never goes away, though, is the trauma etched into the human psyches after the devastation has stormed through an occupied community.

The summer that I was a firefighter, it was an intense fire year. Yet, the national fire situation continues to escalate as climate change strains forest ecosystems that, for much too long, have not been managed using traditional, indigenous methods of forest management. The legacy of fire devastation has continued to stretch my heart almost to its breaking point. There was a devastating wildfire in 1990 in the Foresta community in Yosemite, where one of my friend's homes was incinerated, torching and melting bicycles and cast-iron pans into molten blobs. I was so relieved to learn my friend had not been in her house at the time, though I could not even begin to imagine the enormity of the loss of her possessions and the place where she had called home. In the summer of 2017, when friends of mine lost their homes in Santa Rosa and Sonoma County, I was again reminded of how heartbroken I had been during my time as a firefighter. Day in and day out, I'd had to the face the reality of what fire can do to the mind, body, and soul of a human, and to the scenery, wildlife, and ecology of a habitat. Even without actively fighting a fire, there is no escape—for anyone—from the terror that an out-of-control blaze can ignite.

That summer, we lay next to the fire lines through most nights in the cold, 'babysitting' the fires, making sure they did not jump over our arbitrary boundaries. I tried to ignore how my eyes, nose, and mouth filled with smoke, how the smoke burned my lungs. But I was getting paid to work in a national park, so I told myself I should be grateful.

One night, after a particularly back-breaking day, I could feel the exhaustion settling into my bones. The night sky was pitch-black, the air cold. I flopped myself down, *hard*, onto the ground, my rear landing squarely onto the sharp-edged head of a Pulaski. For a moment, I feared I had cut myself in half. However, somehow, I rolled off the ax head unharmed. After shaking off the shock, I picked myself up, regained my composure, and got back to digging the fire line with renewed energy. I was still alive. The experience had seemed so miraculous I was sure I had been spared for some reason—and I knew that reason was not to continue digging fire lines for the rest of my career. I was a naturalist and a biologist. I wanted to be an educator and to teach people about the natural world, to show them how wondrous it all was, to hope my energy was infectious. That season, my body had been put to the test, but my mind was languishing. Just like my mother had needed more intellectual stimulation in her life, I needed the same.

I was also lonely. That summer, I saw more bears, elk, and coyotes than I saw people. Also, as the only woman on my crew, I felt the pressure trying to prove myself in a male-dominated environment.

At the end of the season, I left my position as a fire fighter. I knew that I did not need to prove to myself or to others that I was strong, or that I was just as capable as the men of enduring the hard work of manual labor.

Firefighting is important work—integral to the health and safety of ecosystems and human communities—but I had learned that it was not the work I was meant to do.

Sometimes grit is having the strength to push forward, even when something is hard. Other times, grit is having the strength to know when pushing forward is not the right choice for you.

3
Be Both Body and Mind

With all my strength, I drove my paddle into the murky water, bracing against gale-force headwinds that threatened to send our canoe backward. That day, I was charged with transporting an eighty-three-year-old man, twenty miles along a waterway in Everglades National Park. The cutoff age for participating in the guided trip was eighty, but the man had lied on his intake form.

I leaned into the wind and plunged my paddle into the water again and again. I had been hired by a canoe outfitter for the winter season that guided people on the hundred-mile Wilderness Waterway. Inwardly, I cursed the old man for lying. Yet, I couldn't blame him. To witness this kind of beauty at water level was perhaps worth a lapse in morals. Each day, we woke early, heading back out onto the water before the wind picked up and the hot sun reached its blazing point. We averaged eight hours of paddling a day until we had reached the 'chickee' huts, which were designated camping platforms in standing water. It was impossible to camp anywhere else, since the forests were impenetrable tangles of mangroves, cacti, and vines, not to mention the strangler fig, which sends out a mess of roots that can engulf an entire host tree.

During the day, I kept my eyes peeled for the shiny backs of dolphins and manatees breaking the surface of the water. I trained my binoculars on flashes of rosy feathers beaming from flamingos, roseate spoonbills, and scarlet ibises.

Though writer and conservationist Marjory Stoneman Douglas had dubbed the Everglades the 'River of Grass', I was beginning to understand how this complex ecosystem was so much more than acres of water and sawgrass. I learned that sawgrass was not even technically a grass, but rather a member of the sedge family. Running my fingers along its edges, I could feel its sharp teeth.

It was in large part due to Marjory Stoneman Douglas's contributions to the understanding of the Everglades that popular opinion began to shift from thinking of the place as a useless swamp to considering it a unique, biologically rich area worth conserving.

Indeed, there were wonders in this place—a pocket of the world where the closer you looked, the more you could see. Home to more than five hundred and fifty species of lichen, the Everglades is an ecosystem where tree trunks are covered in patchworks of color. The willow bustic tree, for example, boasts brilliant red splotches of lichen.

For better or worse, because the Everglades is fed by both freshwater and saltwater, it is the only place in the world where both alligators and crocodiles coexist.

Thirty-nine native orchid species can be found in the park, each one a magnificent display of epiphytic ingenuity. The Everglades hosts a range of epiphytes, or air plants (part of the pineapple family), which are non-parasitic plants that grow on other plants rather than taking root in the ground. They can get by without soil because water and nutrients can be absorbed from the air directly through the leaves of the plant. Some epiphytic plants form hollow chambers that support colonies of acrobat ants.

I was learning the personality of each tree species. Like how, after the yellow-bellied sapsucker pecks holes into the trunk of a West Indies mahogany, insects and hummingbirds flock to the tree to lick up the sap. Or how, when the fruits of the soldierwood tree ripen to be about the size of peppercorns, the fruit explodes and showers to the ground, shooting and scattering the seeds, the sound reminiscent of musket fire. Tree snails trace designs along the bark of wild tamarinds, which are host trees for types of lichen consumed by the snails. The bark pattern of the black mangrove resembles the way drying mud cracks in the sun. Florida's early pioneers burned the bark to use the smoke as a mosquito repellent.

The bald cypress tree can live as long as six hundred years, and spotting one, I would imagine the small miracles such an ancient organism might witness over the span of its life. How many times had it seen a resurrection fern curled by drought—appearing dead and desiccated—waiting until the day it could unfurl and reopen after drinking a tiny amount of water? How many times had it glimpsed the 'queen of the night', the fragrant, white-flowered cactus that opens only after sundown? At dawn, the blossoms close and appear pink. At night, the sweet-smelling flowers attract pollinators like bats, moths, and other insects. Or what about the prickly-pear cactus, with its red cup-shaped blossoms and its purple pear-shaped fruits? Or shoreline sea purslane, a perennial herb with pink flowers that only opens a few hours each day? Has it watched the sea purslane spread itself across sand dunes over centuries, stabilizing the soil and preventing erosion?

When one takes the time to learn about the ecological intricacies of a place, it becomes almost impossible not to see it for the miracle it is.

It was Marjory Stoneman Douglas who observed how the slow movement of shallow sheet flow through sawgrass marshes was an essential mechanism in the ecology of the Everglades. She recognized that the health and preservation of the park depended on the uninhibited flow of water from Lake Okeechobee and Kissimmee River, and that the wanton destruction of wetlands was causing an interruption to the fragile cycle.

That season, I read Douglas's work and dreamed of becoming a conservationist like her. I was absorbed in exactly the kind of intellectual stimulation I had been missing during my firefighting stint at Crater Lake. Not only that, though, I was testing the limits of my body. My arms were muscled and sculpted like they had never been before. My upper body was strong and capable of paddling hours on end.

To be an intrepid woman like Douglas, one had to not only be willing to wade through formidable stacks of books and documents to find the truth of things, one also had to put the body to work and wade through channels matted with seagrass and swat swarms of mosquitoes, bracing against the sun's heat and the wind's teeth.

Somehow, after battling against the relentless headwind all day, we finally reached our chickee for the night. But the struggle was not yet over, because we still had to get my elderly passenger from the boat onto the platform.

"Grab him by the life vest and tug," one guide said.

"Push him from behind!" shouted another.

We heaved and wrangled our weary traveler from the canoe onto the safety of the chickee. After a while, I heard deep, guttural snoring coming from the man's tent.

When the wind finally died down, we cooked dinner over camp stoves. As I hungrily refueled my body, I watched the gentle breeze blowing over miles of lovegrass, arrowfeather, and blackrush. I watched the red-hot sun slip below the horizon line. I batted at mosquitos and listened to the chirps of tree frogs.

Here, sitting at the very tip of the Everglades, the southernmost point of Florida, balanced by the strength of both my brain and my body, I felt nourished.

My body and mind were tested again several years later when I rafted the lower half of the Colorado River through the Grand Canyon. I hitched a ride to the edge of the North Rim and hiked down by myself to meet the boats at Phantom Ranch. From there, we snaked through the black schist walls of the inner gorge, the oldest rock in the canyon, to where we scouted the daunting Crystal Rapid, rated a class ten at the time.

I was in the gear boat with a female guide who did an incredible job making split-second decisions, avoiding constant hazards, and lining up the raft down the rapids. I knew she faced pressure as a female guide to perform—more than the male guides. But at only five feet tall and a hundred pounds, she maneuvered the boat as if she and the river were partners engaged in a dance that they had rehearsed a thousand times. The river led, and she followed, her movements seeming almost effortless—though I knew that they required enormous focus and mental precision. I felt I was in the presence of a true leader, and I took note.

When we entered Crystal Rapid, she yelled, "Highside, highside!"

I flung myself on the right front tube of the raft as we rose up against a massive boulder protruding from the surface of the water. I pushed down with all my might, not wanting to allow the boat to flip and risk losing our gear to the churning river. I felt powerful and useful, throwing my weight and all my strength into this one feat, both mind and body focused on the task at hand.

When the roar of Crystal Rapid faded into the background, I knew we were safely below the belly of the beast. I could feel the tension of the moment ease away, and I even noticed a half smile on my guide's face.

There is something that happens when the mind and body are perfectly in alignment and needle-point focused. Rather than triggering a sense of panic, navigating the crux of the rapid lowered me into a state of peace. It was momentary, but it was there.

The strength of women never ceases to astound me. I think of my mother's body transforming cyclically over the course of twelve pregnancies, and the considerable toughness required to endure that kind of repeated change. I think of my own body and the changes it has been through, and how it is ever shifting. During my time in the Everglades, my upper body became powerful in a way that it never had been before, and hasn't been since.

When I was younger, one of my fantasies was to have a great singing voice. I wanted to belt out songs with my full body like Joni Mitchell or Carole King. I imagined myself sinking into those low notes and lifting into the high ones. Singing seemed the perfect blend of body and mind. Sadly, I cannot carry a tune, though I still did my best to sing lullabies to my sons when they were babies. The closest I ever got to being a musician was falling in love with one during college. He played some covers (think Steely Dan, Bob Marley, and Southern Rock), but mostly originals—some of them love songs. My family would come out to watch his band play and we would dance all night. That was when I learned dancing was the way in which I could still enjoy music in my entire being.

My dreams of becoming a singer did not pan out, but I am grateful to the artists who make music that I can dance to. I love watching Maggie Rogers's music video for her song 'Fallingwater'. In it, she's wearing a flowing red onesie and dancing across giant sand dunes. Her movements are controlled and on tempo, yet you can tell she is releasing herself to the music in full-bodied surrender. When I watch her, I feel free, liberated to dance any way I please, my mind and body feeling perfectly, briefly in sync.

***

On the beach in Corona Del Mar, California, I met a man who pointed to the water.

"See that guy out there? He was a mail carrier in Corona del Mar for thirty years. Now, he's a long-distance swimmer. But before he retired, he walked about twenty miles a day for over thirty years."

I watched the swimmer as his body slid through the water, the rhythm of his strokes even and second-natured. He made the exertion look effortless and invigorating. A rejuvenating reprieve from gravity. It was clear his body had adapted to the challenge of sustaining exercise over long periods of time and I wondered how many miles his body had logged.

I considered the stamina required to accomplish such feats of endurance, for the distance swimmers and runners and cyclists, the ultra-marathoners and thru-hikers. My husband ran the Leadville Trail 100, a grueling hundred-mile backcountry race in Colorado that leads runners through the heart of the Rockies. The course ascends and descends a total of fifteen thousand, six hundred feet, requiring climbing above twelve thousand, six hundred and twenty feet. The race is so taxing on the human body that each year, often only less than half the participants finish the race in the thirty-hour time limit. My husband also ran the Wasatch 100 in the mountains outside Salt Lake City. A friend of ours did a 'double Wasatch', meaning he completed a hundred-mile run with thirty thousand feet in elevation gain and loss and then turned around and ran the same course—another 100 miles—with an equal amount of elevation gain and loss.

There are certain words that come to mind when I think about people who can perform great feats of endurance: determination, perseverance, dedication. But while I think all endurance athletes have some measure of these mindsets, I have come to believe that each one of them possesses a certain special something that distinguishes them from the average person: *grit*.

Researcher Angela Duckworth has done multiple studies on how a high level of grit is the secret ingredient in recipes for success in many high-functioning individuals. Those who are willing and ready to struggle through a task with genuine grit will reap the benefits of their undertakings. Those who scored high on grit surveys demonstrated traits such as higher self-control, mental well-being, resilience, and a mindset that was growth oriented.

What, exactly, constitutes grit? Duckworth's studies have attempted to pinpoint what distinguishes individuals with high levels of grit from the rest of us. One trait she has noticed is the tendency to not give up on tasks when confronted by obstacles. In his book *Hereditary Genius*, Francis Galton posited that personal achievement required intellect as well as 'zeal and the capacity for hard labour'. Within this view, grit is the composite of both cognitive and physical perseverance. Cognitive strengths include the ability to solve problems, learn from experience, reason critically about complex ideas, and plan for the future. The physical components of grit can include speed, agility, and strength. But there is one word in particular that I like the most in Galton's description, which is 'zeal'.

Zeal suggests maintaining a level of enthusiasm (and maybe even love?) that pushes a person to carry forward, even after setbacks, even when the going gets hard (and then harder), even when failure has been the only previous outcome. This passion arms a person with the dedication and perseverance to travel forward and maybe, in time, finally succeed.

Within the physical realm, I am certain that have I have not shown true grit in physical endeavors to the degree that my husband and other endurance athletes have. In my professional life, however, I have achieved all that I set out to do. I was hired by the National Parks Service. I worked in the wilderness. I tested the limits of my body and mind. I became a naturalist and educator, forming connections with people across all walks of life. It required pushing forward even after disappointment, sacrificing certain pleasures in order to pursue certain rewards, and maybe—if I allow myself the credit—even arming myself with a bit of grit.

Part II
Constraints

4
Boundary Lines

I am the only member of my immediate family who has moved west of the Mississippi River.

After majoring in nature recreation and interpretation, with a minor in biology, I graduated in 1986 from the State University of New York at Cortland, then headed west to work with the Student Conservation Association at Grand Canyon National Park as an interpretive naturalist on the South Rim.

Growing up in such a chaotic household with constant company and relentless chatter made me long for the peace and quietude of wide-open spaces. Though I loved my family, I couldn't ignore the pull to start a new life, on my own, in the vast wilderness of the American West.

American newspaper editor Horace Greeley is credited with the phrase 'Go West, young man' in reference to Manifest Destiny, the westward expansion of settlers across North America to claim fertile soil. It was a nineteenth-century belief that the West was fit for people willing to work hard to establish new lives. Now, nearly two centuries after the term 'manifest destiny' was coined, I was answering my own call: 'Go West, young woman'.

Geographically separating myself from my family did not feel like enough, though. To secure a few more degrees of distance, I considered changing my name to create a new, fresh identity that I could use to design a life that would be uniquely my own. It turned out, though, that the tap root of my origins reached deep, and it would have taken quite a bit more resolve to choose a new name entirely. So, I settled instead for a more discreet change. Rather than 'Betty Ann', I started signing my name as 'Bette Anne'—a subtle adjustment. By removing the 'y' in 'Betty', I had put a hard stop in my name. While the 'y' had been an invitation—a soft, easy transition between the beginning and end of my name—replacing it with an 'e' would create an edge. It was abrupt, like the lip of a canyon, delineating a clear boundary between my former life and my future one.

My impulse to give myself a new name after leaving home and encountering a new world was not exactly unique. A couple of years later, Christopher McCandless would hitchhike to Alaska and give himself the new name of 'Alexander Supertramp'. His contagious zeal and zest for life, along with his motivation to live simply and to intimately connect to his surroundings was chronicled in Jon Krakauer's book *Into the Wild*.

Flowing north to south over two thousand, three hundred and forty miles, the Mississippi River bisects the United States. The Ojibwe name for it is *Misi-ziibi*, or 'Great River'. On a map, it is an enormous blue artery—the perfect spatial marker separating east from west, a boundary line so prominent that it is used as a reference point, both geographically and in the mapping of this country's history. In 1803, the Louisiana Purchase doubled the country's territory, pushing it beyond the Mississippi River and further, into land long occupied by First Peoples.

Rivers create natural topographical boundaries, but they are also connectors. The entire Mississippi River drainage basin covers more than one million square miles of this country, meaning that its tributaries fan out like capillaries from the heart of the United States, bridging miles upon miles of ecosystems, linking them all to one water source of origin.

Another iconic American river with its own mythologies and personality is the Colorado, which throws its muscular weight against striations of rock, carving its way southwest across the Colorado Plateau and through the Grand Canyon before entering Mexico. Visitors flock to the Grand Canyon from all over the world to witness its unrivaled beauty, particularly when the park is at its showiest—at sunrise and sunset—when the dull colors of desert are repainted more vibrantly with the brush strokes of low light.

People come for the mega-geology, for the mighty river thrusting through the canyon, for the towering walls, for the immense swath of distinct, layered rock. What is often overlooked, though, are the subtler beauties of the park: the cacti and lichen, the red-spotted toad and short-horned lizard, the fuzzy leaves and the bright orange petal cups of the globemallow.

Sentry milk-vetch is a purple-flowered perennial herb endemic to the area, meaning that Grand Canyon National Park is the only place in the world where this plant resides. It is a plant that has made its home at the edge, growing from the cracks of the Kaibab Limestone, the uppermost layer of rock in the Grand Canyon—standing sentinel over the park. Its species name is *cremnophylax*, which means 'gorge watchman'.

I wondered whether I could make my own way, living on the edge as Bette, straddling the line between the life I wanted and the life I had come from, somehow finding a place in the world that would feel most suitable for me, a place I could call 'home'. Or would a life as a park ranger mean that I would never live anywhere long enough to truly get to know it, to understand its rhythms and the language of a particular landscape? Had I inadvertently chosen a vagabond life like Alexander Supertramp's—a borderless life—where I would drift in and out of places, not staying anywhere long enough to get too comfortable?

My time at the South Rim of the Grand Canyon as a Student Conservation Association (SCA) 'intern' was my official introduction to the National Park Service system. I wore a brown and tan SCA uniform when I greeted travelers at the park visitor center, along with a baseball cap when I led naturalist walks and talks. I was envious of the flat hats, badges, and green-and-gray 'pickle suits' of the *real* park rangers. I aspired to join their ranks someday. While I had made one step in the right direction toward my goal, I realized I still had a long way to go before I could step across the professional threshold that separated me from them.

One day, while working at the South Rim Visitor Center, I met a man with long, brown, feathered hair. He was tall, and irresistibly handsome. Seeing him, I felt pulled, as if I wanted to lean closer to this man standing before me. I could sense an instant attraction between us and hoped I had not imagined it. He introduced himself as Feather.

"Is that your real name?" I asked.

"It is," he said, beaming a huge smile at me.

"It suits you," I said, flirting.

Feather explained that he was a pilot who flew tourists around the canyon rim, but that he spent most of his time in Alaska.

"I would love to take a flight sometime," I said, extending my flirtation further.

Feather took the hint and invited me to see a Taj Mahal concert that night. "I'll pick you up here after you get off of work," he said.

That evening, Feather returned and handed me a small, wooden box that he had carved. Inside the box was a beautiful quartz crystal that he had found in the desert in Arizona. I melted at the thoughtful gift. I would learn that Feather was a rockhound and an accomplished woodworker.

As we made our way to the concert, Feather took my hand and seized my heart. It felt like Taj Mahal was playing just for us, and we danced into the night.

The next day, Feather and I backpacked into the Grand Canyon, descending until we reached the Colorado River, where we waved at boaters and skipped flat stones across the water. We watched rafters jump into the cool river and swim the rolling rapids, laughing through the wild ride. We spent two blissful nights under the stars and spent long, hot days tromping around, spotting rattlesnakes and lizards expertly camouflaged against the brittle desert brush. Feather nicknamed me 'Bright Eyes' and 'Happy One'. There was no way, of course, that I could improve on his name, so I continued calling him Feather.

***

At the end of the spring season as a Student Conservation Association Naturalist at the South Rim, I was hired for my firefighting stint at Crater Lake. Before I left the park, though, I wanted a real adventure. I paid for a spot on a guided trip on the Colorado River from Lees Ferry to Phantom Ranch, so I could run rapids, explore side canyons, and hike through pockets of desert inaccessible from the roads. Because of my association with the park, I felt emboldened to call Martin Litton, a boatman, conservationist, and owner of the world-renowned Grand Canyon Dories. After a brief, sweet conversation, Litton said, "You work in the park, so you're one of us. One of the good ones."

I felt a surge of pride that, even after only a few months, I was *in*. I felt as though I had been admitted to a very exclusive club, one that would afford me experiences I had only dreamed about.

Feather drove me to the put-in at Lees Ferry and begged the boatmen to let him join the trip. "Please, I'll do anything," he pleaded, offering to scrub pots, to cook, to paddle, to row, even cleaning out the 'groover', the fabled portable toilet for such trips. The leader of the trip would not go for it, however, and we pushed off from shore with waves goodbye and apologetic smiles.

We floated to Vasey's Paradise, where we could view stunning vertical microclimates—rock walls covered in lush vegetation, fed from spring water seeping through cracks, waterfalls cascading down fern-covered cliffs.

We spotted the elusive ringtail cat, a member of the raccoon family, characterized by its black and white 'ringed' tail with up to sixteen stripes. Bighorn sheep climbed nimbly up sheer rock faces. Lizards flicked their tongues on rock baking in the sun. Gray flycatchers and pinyon jays swooped in front of us.

After a long, hard day behind the oars of a wooden dory boat, navigating treacherous Class 10 rapids, we needed to decompress. We had been pulling and pushing on oars and paddles all day, swirling around eddies and craggy cliffs. We angled toward shore, then set up camp. At dusk, I listened for the call of the canyon wren, with its descending trill that sounds like a rock falling

    down

    down

    down

the canyon wall. We heard the trill in the evenings and early mornings, a sound that spoke to some primitive ache for connection in a place we were only visiting.

The crystalline Little Colorado River was baby blue against white travertine rock. I swam and floated—mesmerized—along this otherworldly ribbon of water. Blue sky and red rock on all sides. This was the place where the Hopi Indians believed the origin of life emerged from a hole in the bottom of a canyon, or Sipapu. I could sense I was passing through sacred ground.

The next morning, in the pink-gold early morning canyon light, I watched as one of the female guides crawled out of another person's tent—her cheeks rosy, her hair tousled—and I started to miss Feather.

Even surrounded by so much natural beauty and friendly people, I had to acknowledge a certain loneliness—the unsettling kind that manages to work its way into us *even* when we think we are content. While I could strike out alone—leave my family and my former life behind—I still needed connection. I was learning that, to feel whole, I would need to straddle both worlds:

the human and the natural. Without balance, my life might come to feel either too isolating or too stifling. I would need to find ways to nurture both sides in order to satisfy my deep longing for connection.

Seven days later, when we reached Phantom Ranch, I spotted Feather standing in the river. He was grinning and waving frantically. As we approached the takeout, I jumped into the river, and he swam to me and pulled me toward him. We held each other for a long time, until we were certain we had both missed each other equally.

Feather and I said our goodbyes to the river trip crew, then headed up the South Kaibab Trail. As we ascended the hot, steep trail that leads out of the canyon—a vertical mile of elevation gain—we strained under the physical exertion required to lift our tired legs up the dusty incline. Our skin was slick with sweat, our breathing labored. As we climbed, I could sense Feather's concern about my leaving for Oregon soon, which added another type of strain. As much as we had missed each other, I could already feel my own restlessness tugging me away from him. For now, though, I shook the feeling away. For now, the distance had brought us closer together, and I tried removing the mental barrier that was preventing me from leaning fully toward our partnership.

***

Sentry milk-vetch is a threatened species, struggling to survive against the challenges of drought and habitat loss. In 1990, scientists discovered that the sentry milk-vetch near Maricopa Point in Grand Canyon National Park was being trampled by park visitors and that the fragile plant was not bouncing back. Since then, a fence has been positioned between the sentry milk-vetch and park visitors. The plant is now better protected but is much harder to appreciate up close.

How do we engage with beauty without damaging it? How do we foster deep connection—to land, to one another, to ourselves—while still leaving enough room for all to thrive? By moving west of the Mississippi, I had created distance between myself and my family. By going by another name, I had separated myself from my origins. By falling in love with Feather, I could feel myself moving closer to something, while simultaneously resisting that closeness. Without yet knowing it, I was drawing a boundary between myself and him, as if afraid that if I allowed myself to shape a life with him, I would no longer be shaping my own life.

Eventually, I would return to the original spelling of my name. Throughout the course of a life, I have learned, each one of us is in the process of doing one of two things: either returning home or finding a home within ourselves.

5
More Afraid of Strangers than Wildlife

"Betty Ann, we know you can put on your hiking boots and function just fine in the outdoor world," my college professor Dr. Young said. "Now, it may be time to learn how to put on the professional shoe. You need to learn to be comfortable with a foot in both worlds."

After college, before heading out West, I was offered an esteemed position as intern with an affiliate of the National Park Service. After hearing my professor's words of encouragement, I accepted an intern position with the National Parks Conservation Association (NPCA) in Washington, D.C.

I lived at American University and commuted by bus or bicycle down Embassy Row to my office, reminding myself each day that I was a part of something bigger than myself, and I framed that period of time through a romantic lens. I was thrilled to finally be officially involved with the parks, preservation, and conservation movement.

I recalled my first day of class with Dr. Young, an astute professor who would become my mentor. As we students sat down at our desks that first class, pulling out copies of Roderick Nash's *Wilderness and the American Mind*, Dr. Young began tossing magazines from various environmental organizations toward us. He flung the publications this way and that, pages fluttering in the air like a flock of pigeons. A few landed on my desk, then fell to the floor. I picked them up and flipped through each one: *Sierra Club*, *The Nature Conservancy*, and *National Geographic*. Meanwhile, my professor gesticulated wildly. He was animated, excited.

"These organizations are working hard to protect the lands that we love," he said. "The environmental movement is a big deal and it's happening right now. It's important work, and it will be a huge part of our coursework."

His energy was infectious. I flipped through the glossy pages of each publication, picturing myself contributing something to the greater cause of protecting the environment. In a flurry of enthusiasm, Dr. Young had already convinced me to be a crusader for our national parks and wild spaces. Through his passion, he got me to recognize that the organizations committed to protecting the environment and educating the public were an integral part of American culture.

Living in D.C., a sense of loyalty and dignity grew in me as I attended Senate and congressional hearings on environmental issues. I researched and wrote for NPCA's magazine and newsletters. I visited every museum. At times, I felt like a fish out of water having moved from rural Upstate New York to the inner city of Washington, D.C., but I made the most of my time. I met friends of friends from SUNY's School of Environmental Forestry in Syracuse, one of whom was an arborist and 'tree doctor', helping treat and save some of D.C.'s most beautiful trees. We attended outdoor concerts at Wolf Trap Park for Performing Arts, listening to Bonnie Raitt's and B.B. King's voices belt out into the thick, heavy D.C. humidity. Years later, I would listen closely to the lyrics of Bonnie Raitt's song 'Nick of Time', and truly appreciate how, eventually, I would find love, and ultimately a family—just in the nick of time.

For now, though, I was trying to appreciate my time as a single woman in a big city. I had grown up having seven strong, strapping, protective brothers around, helping me to feel safe. Here, I was left to my own devices, and consequently left to make my own discernments about potentially compromising situations.

One gloriously sunny spring day, I jumped off my commuter bus to walk to a friend's place. On my way, a tall, elegant gentleman approached me. "I can't find my car," he said in my direction.

I looked around and noticed how we were the only two people in the quiet, suburban D.C. neighborhood, cars lining both sides of the street. "What does it look like?" I asked. "What color is it?"

"It's white," he said. "A BMW." It would only be much later that I would realize this piece of information was meant to impress me.

"Well, that doesn't help me," I said. "I have no idea what type of car that is."

"Don't worry, I'll find it." He paused, looked at me, and smiled. "What are you up to?"

I was house-sitting for a friend but wasn't sure whether or not to go into details. I hemmed and hawed.

"I live right over here," he said, waving vaguely down the street.

"Oh, cool. What do you do in this crazy city?" I asked.

"I'm a solar lobbyist with the U.S. government. I travel the world and attend meetings on solar energy. I just got back from Japan. I attended a conference and took some beautiful photographs. Would you like to see them sometime?"

"Sure," I said. "Here is my phone number. Give me a shout a little later." With that, I skipped off.

Later, I received his call. He gave me the address to his place, and I met him there to watch the slideshow. It wasn't until I stepped into his apartment, looked around, and noticed how alone with him I felt that I became nervous. He had set up a slide projector situated in such a way that the photos had to be viewed from his queen bed. I sat on the bed, my body rigid, listening to this older man narrate his slideshow.

He seemed kind, and I did enjoy his presentation on the cultural diversity and solar energy of Japan. He talked about his older friends and how one of them was having a 'coming out' party because she was getting a divorce and wanted to throw a bash to let everyone know she was single. I was so young and inexperienced in matters of marriage—let alone divorce—that I was truly rapt. After all, I was a newly graduated young woman without any married friends.

Once I had begun trusting this man, he confided in me. "I wasn't really looking for my car when I met you. I knew where it was, down the street."

My stomach lurched. It was not so much that I was afraid of this particular man, but that I was suddenly fearful of the circumstances that my naivete could lead me into. I was unsettled by how my instinct to trust people could be used against me—that I could be taken advantage of by simply being helpful, friendly, and wide-eyed.

Even after I thought I had attained some city savvy, I still found myself in situations where I had to negotiate my safety with the unwanted attention of men. I instructed the security attendant at the dorm office at American University to not allow a certain individual entrance to the building, since I could not reciprocate this person's feelings for me. However, my unwanted guest appeared at my dorm room, anyhow.

"How did you get in here?" I asked him as he stood in my door.

"I just gave some excuse and they believed me," he replied.

"I have work to do."

"Come on, baby," he said. "You ain't ever gonna get this lucky again."

"I'm not up for company," I said. "I have some writing to do for work, and you need to go."

"You sure I can't come in?" he said, now trying to wriggle past the doorway and into the room. I faced him, standing resolute and on guard, my body a barrier between him and my quiet night alone.

He left, but I was shaken.

As I grew older, I ventured out on many solo backpacking trips, along with innumerable day hikes in the backcountry out West. Most of the time, I did not feel fearful. Only rarely did a wildlife encounter make me shudder. On occasion, though, meeting another human in the backcountry would stop me cold in my tracks.

On a solo trip in the San Juan Mountains outside Telluride, Colorado, I was camping about eleven thousand feet above sea level. I slept peacefully and woke up to sunshine glistening on dew-covered grasses, lupine, and larkspur in a high alpine meadow. I heard rustling nearby and decided to investigate. I climbed out of my sleeping bag half-dressed, in a long T-shirt and no shorts, thinking no one would be around. One hundred yards from my tent I saw a herd of forty elk—mostly cows and calves. Entranced by their presence, I followed them for an hour, over the course of a quarter mile, and watched them busily eating the fresh, new green vegetation. They ignored me, and I was able to soak in one of those rare moments in nature when one feels isolated and connected at once. After a while, I got hungry and returned to my tent.

As I lay half in, half out in my tent, I heard more noise. This time, it was of the human variety. I bolted upright, seeing that a sheepherder had crept up next to my tent.

"You got any weed?" he asked.

"No," I replied, trying to keep my voice calm, although I felt as though melting ice were trickling down my spine.

The man continued asking for things in a demanding way. He was heavy-set, with a thick black mustache, his body hunched in a way that made me assume that lurking was a common activity of his.

"Beer?"

I felt compelled to explain that I would never carry heavy cans of beer in my pack two thousand feet up a mountain, but I resisted. "No," I said, annoyed now.

"You got any cigarettes?"

I had never smoked a cigarette in my life. "Nope." I was growing more agitated, unsure what I could say to convince him to leave.

The man lingered, twisting his mustache in his fingers and glaring at me.

Panicked now, I scrambled to pack up all of my gear, tearing my tent down, stuffing my belongings haphazardly into my backpack. Sweating, heart racing, I ran all the way down the mountain and straight into the sleepy town of Telluride. By the time I reached the safety of a public space, I was gasping, my heart pounding out of my chest.

After that, I was less keen on solo-backpacking, but I still ventured out alone overnight on occasion.

***

I was learning that to straddle both worlds—the professional and the natural world—would require learning how to protect myself in each. I was not sure if I was more afraid of brown bears and snakes than I was of the men in the city and in the wilderness. To forge ahead on the path I had chosen would mean to stay alert. In the years to come, I would learn to read the signs. The signs were there, I just needed to know how to identify them. The warning sound of a snake's rattle. The unsettling gaze of a stranger. I had entered the environmental movement with a sense of bright-eyed wonder and excitement, and now that was being tempered with the troubling realization that I would be doing dangerous work. I was not deterred, but I resolved to move forward more cautiously, acknowledging the constraints imposed by my female body, while also recognizing that in my body was its own protective measure. In the coming years, my career would shape my body into its fittest form. I would learn how to keep myself safe in wild spaces. I would learn how to handle myself around the men in my field, but I would also hold tightly to my wide-eyed, dreamy passion for the environmental movement. I discovered that I could be both a strong woman and a park ranger who preserved her child-like wonder for the natural world. That my life did not have to be limited by any constraints placed on my body and mind, nor did my hopes and passions need to be reduced.

6
Bridging the Gap Between Us and Wilderness

To learn how to be a good steward of wild spaces means to understand how to peaceably and respectfully coexist with the wild beings who call those places home. It is to understand that, while humans are wild creatures too, at this point in our evolution we are often only passing through wild spaces. We are guests in someone else's home.

One summer, for a backcountry course required for graduation, a professor took me and other students into the Five Ponds Wilderness Area in the Adirondack Mountains. Attentively, I listened to him discuss wilderness ethics and backcountry protocol, emphasizing his high expectations that his students adhere to these guidelines.

One night, while I was off on a solo activity in the field, my professor snuck into my tent and discovered a tube of toothpaste in my backpack. When I returned, I was severely scolded.

"You know that bears have a strong sense of smell and can detect this scent from miles away!" he yelled.

"You should know better. This is something we talked about in minimum impact camping class." He was not kidding around, and I worried about getting a grade deduction for the wilderness component of the class, blowing my stellar 4.0 cumulative grade point average. I hung my head, apologizing over and over. At that moment, I was more frightened of my professor than I was of a black bear.

I aced the class *and* I also never stowed my toothpaste in my tent again.

Another mistake that will forever make me cringe was the time Feather and I were road tripping along the San Andreas fault in a Volkswagen bus from Crater Lake to Baja Mexico after my firefighting stint. A native Californian, Feather navigated through the state along dirt roads to remote, pristine lakes, where we would camp without having to pay a penny. We ate avocado and tomato sandwiches along with Feather's incredible guacamole and chips. We stopped in every natural hot spring along the way, soaking in the calming water, and slept in the van at the end of each day.

One freezing morning at dawn, we heard a *rap, rap, rap* on the steamed-up window of the bus. Startled, we looked out the window to see a National Park Service ranger peering in at us. The ranger informed us that we were parking and camping illegally.

"Please pack up and be on your way," he said politely.

Red-hot shame burned through my body, and I blushed. As a fellow park ranger, I had a code of honor to uphold, and I was embarrassed to be caught disobeying NPS rules. I was also unsettled to notice the ranger's gun. While I loved being an NPS ranger, I knew I would never get my law enforcement commission and carry a firearm. Packing a gun only seemed to invite a mentality of looking for trouble in the parks.

I was a ranger naturalist who wanted to teach people about the natural world. Growing up, I had been antagonized by the police while hanging out in the woods with friends. One time, while sitting on the curb of the school parking lot, minding my own business, a patrol car had pointed its headlights at me, blinding me. I'd held up a hand to shield my eyes from the glare.

"Young lady, what's your name?" the officer asked.

"Jane Russell," I announced.

The officer smirked. "Okay, sure. Whatever you say. But isn't that the name of a bra model?"

Now, with the ranger waiting for Feather and me to leave, I did not feel any urge to be cheeky with law enforcement. As a ranger, it would be my responsibility to uphold the rules and regulations that had been put in place to protect our national parks. I would just go about it without a gun.

***

Humans can do deranged things and a healthy fear around certain people is advisable. But when it comes to wild animals, I am more curious than afraid. Reports of mountain lion sightings in areas where I have lived have been unsettling, but that has not kept me from continuing to explore those wild spaces.

One time, a friend was biking up a dirt road in Colorado and sensed something close behind her. As she swung around to look, there was a mountain lion loping toward her. Adrenaline rushed through her, pushing her to pedal faster up the road, her legs pumping, heart racing. She looked to her right and saw another mountain lion on the side of the road, crouching in the brush. She biked farther up the road, panting and sweating now. When she reached the top of a hill, she looked around cautiously. Not seeing any mountain lions within view, she stopped and called her husband, requesting that he please come pick her up immediately. "I cannot bike home right now, my legs are shaking too much," she told him.

A few days later, I walked on the same road and the same fearless friend was out for a run.

After living in Colorado for more than twenty years, I finally saw my first mountain lion. I was walking through my neighborhood, a quarter of a mile from my house, when I saw a flash of a long tail. I had not been sure that I had seen a mountain lion though, so I got out of my car and bent over to examine huge pawprints in the snow. Unmistakable. A large mountain lion was roaming my neighborhood. Later, another neighbor would report that she had spotted a mountain lion in her backyard while her Bernese Mountain dog puppy watched from the window.

Wildlife biologists are unsure what continues to bring mountain lions in closer proximity to humans in recent years—whether it has to do with an overabundance of prey populations such as rabbits and rodents down in the valley that attract predators like mountain lions to descend from the high country to lower elevations, or possibly a particularly difficult winter resulting in a challenging hunting season. On this, I feel mixed emotions. Admittedly, it felt exhilarating to catch a glimpse of this magnificent mammal who reigns at the top of the food chain. Spotting tracks in the snow is not as magical as seeing a wild cat slip away like a shadow in the night. However, their increasing proximity to humans makes these big cats more susceptible to the threats and constraints that our species can impose on them. While I'm always secretly hoping to see evidence of mountain lions in the places where I live, I'm also simultaneously hoping that they keep well away—more for their own protection than for mine. Big cats losing fear of humans will mean that humans might become more fearful of these muscled, sharp-toothed predators, and decide to remove them from the area in the name of 'safety'. As a wildlife advocate and educator, this has been one of the most difficult paradoxes to navigate: to protect both human life and wildlife—how keeping humans safe sometimes means removing potentially dangerous threats like big cats, and black and brown bears. It is difficult to ignore how our neighborhoods are encroaching on the home of the mountain lion. But as humans, we flip the narrative and argue that mountain lions are entering *our* territory when they wander into our neighborhoods. Sometimes, mutual respect between species means maintaining a safe distance.

***

Bridging the gap between humans and wilderness can look like learning more about what connects the two. Let me tell you about my love affair with the cattail reed plant.

The birthplace of much young love, college was where it began. I was asked to do a project in my field natural history class, and I needed to create a display worthy of the nature center, so I chose to research the cattail reed. As a kid, I had grown up drying them, trying to smoke them, playing with the seeds. I knew that it was possible to make a kind of pancake out of the flour, or to eat the cucumber-like tubers as a delicacy. I knew the cattail was an important plant to Native people of the region, and I wanted to further my peers' education on this versatile plant.

Cattails grow in swamps, wetlands, and wet thickets, easily spotted for their brown, cigar-shaped seed heads, which contain thousands of tiny seeds. When fully grown, cattails can reach six feet tall, with long, grass-like, linear leaves.

First Peoples wove mats out of cattails, using them as features in wigwams, and to eat, sit, or sleep upon. They would also braid cattail reeds into baskets, belts, bags, and straps. The fluffy down of the cattail seed heads was collected to use as insulation for clothing, footwear, and even for stuffing diapers and padding a baby's cradleboard. The tight seed heads keep the down dry, even after rain, making the fluff not only an excellent insulator but also a useful resource for tinder to build fires.

Tribes would snack on the inner core flesh. I gathered cattail reeds and tubers, dried them, pulverized them into flour, and made a type of cattail mush that Native people ate as a staple, or to treat abdominal cramps and coughs. It was also used as a toothpaste. I learned how the starchy, sticky sap between the leaves can be added to soups and broths as a thickening agent. The white shoots at the base of the leaves can be boiled, steamed, or eaten raw. Consuming the young flowerheads or adding flour from the root to hot water could be used to treat dysentery.

I learned how cattail pollen is both hemostatic and astringent, meaning it can be applied directly to a wound to control bleeding or ingested to reduce internal bleeding, menstrual pain, and chest pain. The pounded root can be used as a poultice to treat infections, insect bites, and blisters. The sticky starch of the leaf base is an antiseptic, a coagulant, and has numbing properties.

I constructed a poster board describing the use of the life-giving cattail reed and passed around parts of the plant to my classmates. An effective way to teach natural history is to incorporate all five senses. We sampled the buttery inner flesh of the fresh spring sprouts—sweet and delicious. With our fingertips, we brushed against the soft, plush seed head. We smelled the wet, damp earth around the marsh. We trekked out to where the cattails grew and heard the song of the red-winged blackbirds as they claimed their territory and mated. Like the early people, the red-winged blackbirds were master weavers and wove the reeds into beautiful nests in which to rear their young.

By acquiring knowledge about the natural world, we learn that it is not a separate world from ours, but that the human world and natural world have long been intertwined, that humans have been interconnected with the environment for centuries, and that it has only been in recent human history that we have fractured ecosystems, separated ourselves from the wilderness, and insulated ourselves from that which also makes us wild. For me, cattails provide a reminder of our current dissociation and our historic connectedness. Without intimate knowledge of their anatomy, habitat, and uses, we might simply overlook this plant as just another swamp reed, nothing more.

7

'The National Parks: America's Best Idea'

The National Parks Service is mandated with a delicate balancing act. Somehow, it must work to preserve the parks for future generations while also managing them for their current use and enjoyment—an almost Sisyphean task.

Upon arriving in Washington D.C., I felt surges of pride and commitment to the Park Service, especially after meeting Jonathan Jarvis, who would later become the director of the U.S. National Park Service, the man who stood behind the notable fact that the national parks had begun as a unique American idea. As the documentary filmmaker Ken Burns portrayed in his stunningly beautiful series, 'The National Parks: America's Best Idea', we were on to something special. With the establishment of the National Parks Service in 1916 and the Wilderness Act and the Antiquities Act, the U.S. trailblazed a model that has allowed flocks of people to enjoy some of the most beautiful wild spaces in the country, while also protecting these areas indefinitely. At NPCA in D.C., I worked with people who were emboldened by a deep passion to serve the precepts of conservation and preservation. I had studied Roderick Nash's *Wilderness and the American Mind*, Everett Ruess's *A Vagabond for Beauty*, Aldo Leopold's *A Sand County Almanac*, and, of course, Edward Abbey's *Desert Solitaire*, along with many other works by the great nature writers, including the transcendentalist Thoreau. But, as I continued my education, I learned that early government legislators and park administrators were often only interested in preserving America's most sensational landmarks: the Grand Canyon, the Grand Tetons, Mount Rainier, Mount Saint Helens, Mount Lassen, Zion, Bryce, Canyonlands—places with unmatched, otherworldly scenery. Government officials seemed to preserve only what was most extraordinary, not seeming to consider conserving whole home ranges of wildlife or keeping ecosystems intact.

The more I learned, the more I discovered that there was an evolution to preserving our national parks. I learned that while it was, perhaps, 'America's Best Idea', it was maybe more accurate to say that the parks were built on America's Best *Ideas*. The more I read, the more I discovered that national decisions surrounding conservation were the product of a complex—and ever-shifting—set of discoveries, conversations, and research. During the initial stages of the founding of the National Park Service, 'natural resource managers' (for which there was not yet an official title), were looked to for their knowledge of the critical importance of preserving whole home ranges and ecosystems for wildlife. Ecologists like Aldo Leopold were integral in the shaping of environmental philosophies. He advocated for treating the Earth with a regard for 'deep ecology', an idea that encourages seeing all living beings as fundamental to the health of the planet, regardless of their perceived use. His ecological ethic rejected the notion of human supremacy over all other forms of life, and his advocacy for this approach influenced land use decisions that led to the return of mountain lions and bears to wilderness areas in New Mexico. He was not afraid to disagree with conservation efforts if they diverged from the fundamental theories in which he believed. For example, despite Theodore Roosevelt's commitment to conservation, Leopold opposed Roosevelt's utilitarian approach. It was this dimension of U.S. environmental history that so intrigued me: how even the most outspoken and influential environmental advocates could agree on the fundamentals of preservation, yet disagree on the proper implementation of policy. It was the necessity of ongoing dialogue that made me want to be part of the conversation.

I enjoyed how environmental science could be so dynamic—how there was always room for theories to be disproved or revised. One classic example is the disagreement between preservationist John Muir and the chief of the California Geological Survey, Josiah

Whitney, on the geologic processes that formed Yosemite Valley. John Muir did not finish his coursework at the University of Wisconsin, instead heading out west to the 'University of the Wilderness'. Muir studied the landscape of Yosemite Valley, suspecting that it was surely the product of glacial carving, noting the hanging valleys, striations, erratics, and other geologic phenomenon that seemed characteristic of glacial activity. In Alaska, he had observed similar glacial features that showed correlations with those of Yosemite. Josiah Whitney, on the other hand, argued that the notable rock formations had been the result of a cataclysmic sinking of the valley floor, calling Muir a 'mere sheepherder' and an 'ignoramus'.

It is one thing to debate the theory of the formation of a landform, but it is quite another matter to debate the best approach for how to conserve that landform most responsibly. When it comes to land use issues, there is often much debate, particularly when it comes to how much regulation is necessary to keep wilderness pristine and ecosystems healthy, while also allowing humans to enjoy wild spaces so that they might invest more in the protection of them.

Recreational climbing in the U.S. was born on federal public land. Originally viewed as a vagabond fringe sport, it was left largely unregulated. However, the advancement of climbing gear and the activity's increased popularity brought climbing into the mainstream conversation about land use, regulation, and accessibility. In the 1930s, climbers began scaling the prominent rock faces within Yosemite National Park, and by the mid-1950s, climbing equipment and techniques had advanced enough that word got out that Yosemite was a climbing mecca.

From 1988 to 1992, I taught environmental education for Yosemite Institute (now NatureBridge) in the national park, with a band of twenty-five other like-minded individuals. I could often be found at Sunnyside Campground or Camp 4, visiting with international climbers within an atmosphere of merrymaking—outdoor enthusiasts coming together in a climber's paradise. The mood was often light and celebratory. We were a constant carnival of people bouldering, slacklining, kicking around a hacky sack, and flinging frisbees. Free and wild spirits coming together in the Sierra Nevada. Camp 4 was the place to meet up with climbers via a message board, many taking a risk to match with a good climbing partner, something I gambled with on occasion. One day, I paired up with a Norwegian who spoke marginal English and demonstrated zero fear of heights, and occasionally I climbed with a man who lived in a blue bakery truck and worked for search and rescue. He would free solo climb above me, nailing me with rocks, and I tried to suppress my fear that at any moment he might fall and pull me off the belay ledge. These were all details that I never shared with my mother.

In summer, we climbed on long, warm, sunny days, the granite cool and solid against our hands, not crumbling or flaking off. My first week in Yosemite, a friend invited me to hike up to the base of a sheer granite face named Washington's Column. My friend had invited another person along, and the three of us scrambled over giant boulders strewn across a talus field at the base of the rock face. After spending all day talking and adventuring, we returned to the valley floor. My friend and I parted ways with our tall, fit, blond, mild-mannered companion. After he had left, my friend turned to me in Degnan's Deli and said, "You don't know who that is, do you?"

"Not a clue," I said.

"That's climbing legend John Bachar, one of the world's best big wall climbers. He's a free climber, an all-around American icon."

The John Bachar I came to know was my next-door neighbor in Foresta, the community where I lived in Yosemite National Park. He wore tube socks and T-shirts and cut-off jean shorts. I would listen to him playing his saxophone in the yard, the music drifting up through the canopy of live oak and Ponderosa pine boughs.

Though I would learn that this climbing machine of a man had earned some of the most notable climbing achievements of his time—including a link up of both El Capitan and Half Dome in only fourteen hours, and free soloing Enterprise—my relative unfamiliarity with rock climbing at the time did not allow me to fully gauge his extremism.

Back down in the Yosemite Valley one day, I heard some commotion. I looked over to see John Bachar engaged in an altercation with another prominent climber. There was chest poking, shoving, and maybe even some punching attempts. They were debating one of the longest-running, most divisive philosophical disputes within the climbing community: to bolt or not to bolt.

"Don't chop my bolts," I heard the one who was not Bachar say.

Bolting is a safety technique in climbing that involves drilling anchors into the rock face to protect climbers from long falls. Fixed anchors (at the top of a route) are necessary for safe climbing and are a 'fixed' or permanent feature of a route, used by both traditional and sport climbers. Bolts, on the other hand, are depended on by sport climbers, and are glued or drilled into the rock face along the entire route, which allows for more safety, and also broadens the range in which sport climbers can test their physical limits, since they do not have to stop repeatedly during an ascent to place temporary gear. Traditional climbing, by contrast, emphasizes a pristine, natural wilderness experience over athleticism, leaving minimal traces of the activity on the rock's features. Most safety equipment is temporarily placed and then removed while climbing a traditional route. Some view traditional climbing as more 'old school', and limiting in terms of the safety and athleticism it allows. In order to secure more safety and comfort, some climbers go so far as to file down sharp rock edges, scrub lichen from the surface, and fill loose holds with epoxy or resin. Traditionalists view bolting as fundamentally against the wilderness ethics of climbing, stripping the rock of its natural aesthetics and unnecessarily altering a natural landscape to accommodate a sport. Some debates on the topic can get heated, as was now the case with Bachar and the other climber.

Whether a person engages in sport climbing or traditional climbing, there is no doubt that both leave their mark on the wilderness. The social nature of the sport means that a high density of human activity can congest natural areas. Climber trails—often poorly planned and excessively numerous—erode soil and raze flora, which can affect water runoff and impact water quality. Human commotion in the staging areas near rock walls can impose on the wildlife that roost, nest, and breed in or near rocky features. Inadvertent encroachment on, or even blatant disregard, for Native sacred sites has also become increasingly problematic.

What was clear in the bolting issue tussle was that these were two philosophically opinionated climbers. And perhaps their elite status meant that their arguments and their conviction were that much stronger and their potential influence that much greater. While their school of thought on the subject differed, one main commonality on which they could agree: their relentless love for the sport. Neither one of them was arguing that all climbers should abandon their beloved activity in the name of wilderness preservation. Thus, one thing was clear, which was that it would be the responsibility of climbers and the task of land use regulators to shape behavior in such a way that would limit the damage to the places where climbers want to climb. This raised an even stickier philosophical question: is it possible for humans to immerse themselves in nature without causing harm to the environment?

I worked in Shasta-Trinity National Forest as a climbing ranger in 1992, patrolling the dispersed campgrounds on the slopes of the stunning volcanic peak that people traveled from near and far to see. Some visitors believed that there were special forces at work on Mount Shasta, including spaceship landings from the lenticular clouds and extraterrestrial sightings. These folks were usually harmless except for the fact that they did not often understand all the finer points of minimum impact camping. They would dig trenches around their flimsy tents to divert rainwater from flooding their lair, which would disturb native plants and the fragile soils. They would build medicine circles, removing large rocks and placing them in a 'spiritual' zen-like garden. Unfortunately, this often-killed plants and made for an unnatural looking man-made landscape. It took careful education to teach these visitors that they were having a destructive—not constructive—impact on the environment.

While many ecologists, educators, policy makers, and outdoor enthusiasts agree on the fact that protecting the wild spaces is of critical importance, it is often the approach about which they disagree. This is what makes environmental protection so tricky—and what also makes it so endlessly interesting. It is this core dilemma that has kept me coming back to the conversation, because, in my experience, it is often conversation that is more productive than any debate.

Part III
Love and Loss

8
A Daughter Lost at Sea

My father wanted to be a veterinarian, so as a teenager, he worked at my Aunt Betty's in-laws' farm, tending to the cattle and other animals. One day, my mother, who was fifteen at the time, was sitting at the kitchen table when in walked a tall, handsome nineteen-year-old with thick, wavy brown hair. My mother said it was love at first sight. To come see my mother and visit the farm, my father would walk four miles each way. My mother and father were married by the time my mom turned eighteen.

My father was unable to finish veterinarian school due to the cost and the time commitment. Instead, he worked at General Electric so he could support his family, which was quickly growing. Before long, he was the proud father of twelve children.

On summer days, he would take us on outings in the forest. For snacks, he packed malt balls, hot dogs, and marshmallows. While his children ran wild in the woods for a few hours, he would sharpen sticks for roasting hot dogs and marshmallows over the fire. As a game, my father would tie a tin pie pan to a tree and members of the family would take turns target shooting with a BB gun.

When my father wasn't working and my mother wasn't tending to children, my parents toiled in the garden, spending hours tilling the loamy, fertile soil. On Sundays, the family would have a barbecue and picnic in our backyard. Sometimes, we would add ripe tomatoes and fresh greens from the garden to the menu. I loved the tomatoes, warm and juicy, straight from the vine on a hot August day, laden with mayonnaise or simply eaten plain with a dash of salt.

Not only did my father spend his time parenting his many children, but he also influenced hundreds of local boys by running the baseball program. He coached teams that my brothers played for and became president of the Eastwood Baseball Little League.

Most of my memories of my father have been handed to me by my siblings, filling the blanks for moments when I might have been too young to remember all the ways in which he loved us. When I was six years old, my father was diagnosed with lung cancer. Soon after, my youngest sister was born. My parents named her Christine since she was born four days before Christmas.

Six months after my father's lung cancer diagnosis, my mother sent my older and closest sister and I to our Aunt Betty's home. One evening, she and I were soaking in the bathtub. The water had grown cold by the time Aunt Betty popped her head inside the door. Seeing the look on her face, I froze. I had never seen someone's face look like that before, and I was scared. My sister's gaze followed mine.

"What is it?" I asked.

Aunt Betty knelt down so that her eyes were level with ours. My stomach seized. This was not good.

I wanted to freeze time. I wanted to run from the room so that I would never have to hear what she was about to say.

"I have something very sad to tell you," she said. "Your dad has died."

My sister and I had been playing in the relaxing bubble bath when our world's biggest bubble burst. My huge family was now fatherless.

For days, I was hysterical, screaming and crying. I felt so alone, so scared, so worried for my family. Night after night, I cried myself to sleep. Meanwhile, my mother did her best to make arrangements, while also tending to the emotional needs of a family gutted by loss. Privately, she mourned the loss of her only true love. She never remarried.

Even at only six years old, I still felt the weight of what was happening falling heavily upon me as I tried to comprehend what it would be like to live in the world without my father. Who was going to take us camping in the woods? Who would play baseball, roast hotdogs over the fire, or plant vegetable gardens?

The ballpark where my father had coached was named after him when he passed away. The photos of the dedication ceremony show a family that looked both proud and shell shocked.

In the wake of my father's death, I was left with more questions than answers. As I grew older, the only thing I became certain of was that I had inherited my father's love of nature and spending time outdoors. I had no doubt in my mind that the camping trips we had taken as a family had led me to pursue a career in the outdoors. My father's career was derailed, and his life was cut short. I will never be sure whether my dogged determination to work for the National Parks Service was my way of becoming a surrogate for my father's thwarted ambitions. Nevertheless, the natural world became an integral part in the healing of my heart. Before I left home, I would often find myself exiting our chaotic, noisy house, seeking refuge and quiet in the woods. As a teenager, when I imagined myself growing into adulthood, I conjured images of myself finding peace in wild spaces. Without my father, being in nature would be a way for me to feel whole. I would seek activities like hiking, fishing, camping, and studying field natural history to feel closer to my father. Throughout my life, there have been many moments in wild spaces when I have felt the therapeutic and curative power of nature seep into my mind, body, and spirit, and it is in these moments that I feel my father's presence— not so much surrounding me but shining out from within.

***

On my road trip with Feather, we headed south from Crater Lake toward Klamath Falls and Lassen National Park. Our destination was Paradise, California. Driving through that lovely town, it would have been unfathomable for me to imagine that in 2018, twenty-six people would lose their lives and thousands of homes would be swallowed by a forest fire. Feather's parents lived in Paradise, and I was nervous to meet the people who had raised my constant companion, hoping they would accept me. All my worries fell away, though, when they welcomed me with open arms. However, it was strange to be around Feather's father, since I had grown up without one. Hearing stories about all the trips Feather and his dad had taken to explore the West, I noticed a hot envy scorching my insides, and I secretly wished my dad had been alive long enough to go on such adventures with me.

Feather noticed a shift in my demeanor and asked how I was doing.

"I feel unsure how to be around your dad," I said. "It hurts my heart. I miss my dad."

"I'm so sorry," Feather said, holding me in a long embrace. "I wish you'd never lost him, or that I could bring him back to you."

In that moment, I felt grateful that even though I had lost the most important man in my life much too young, I had somehow managed to find another important man. However, I knew that no matter how good a man Feather was, he could never be the missing piece that had been ripped from my heart after my father died.

At the end of a lovely visit, Feather and I said goodbye to his parents, and made our way south to Yosemite National Park. It was my first time visiting the park, and I did my best to absorb the sweeping views of glaciated granite, imagining what it must have been like for John Muir to behold this place his first time, becoming so familiar with its curves and striations that he could develop a hypothesis about its creation. I craned my neck to take in the mammoth rock formations. I pressed my nose in between the craggy bark tiles of Jeffrey pine trunks to inhale the vanilla-like scent. I knelt to brush my hands over the subalpine wildflower meadows bedazzled with monkeyflowers, lupine, and shooting stars. Spending even a brief time in the park, something lit up inside me, and I felt connected to this place that had, until now, been unknown to me. Little did I know that I would soon return to the park to teach environmental education for four years.

After leaving the Sierra mountains, we drove west, finally reaching the California coast. We wandered to the edge of a cliff, and for the first time in my life, I took in a view of the Pacific Ocean. I gasped at the sight, absorbing the never-ending expanse of blue water spreading out before me. I smelled the salty air and felt the warm, wet breeze blowing through my long hair. The humidity put wave into my normally straight locks. I relished the way this moisture made me feel, and the way that sea level gifted my lungs and body with more oxygen. It was noticeable how much easier it was to breathe here than up in the high Sierra Nevada mountain range. Energized, I hugged Feather and kissed him hard.

"Thank you for sharing this with me," I said. Although I had never been to the Pacific Ocean before, I felt as if I was home.

I did not think that I could feel any more joyful, but standing on the cliff in a warm embrace, Feather and I looked out across the ocean and saw gray whales rising to the surface. They paused there, then sank back down into the salty blue. Again, I gasped.

Several years later, I would be offered a position as a naturalist on a historic wooden sailing vessel that traveled around the Turnagain Arm, a waterway in the Gulf of Alaska. During my research, I would learn that gray whales (the same species Feather and I had seen off the California coast) can weigh up to 40 tons and can grow to a length of forty-five feet. They are only found in the Pacific Ocean. As migrators, they travel in groups called pods, often swimming a twelve thousand, four hundred and thirty mile-round trip from their summer home in Alaska to the warmer waters of the Mexican coast.

Despite their incredible attributes, gray whales are not the darling of marine biology. In the early 1990s, I met a whale biologist who memorably told me that, "Gray whales are bottom-feeding slugs."

Because he was so attractive, passionate, and convincing, I hung on every word he said. He was not wrong about gray whales' bottom-feeding behavior. They spend their days rolling on their sides, sucking sediment and invertebrates from the sea floor. They swim slowly, filtering food between their baleen plates, trailing long clouds of mud behind them. Still, there was a part of me that felt almost slighted by the disparaging way in which this handsome biologist painted gray whales. He was busy studying the charismatic humpback whales whose natural history and feeding behaviors were, admittedly, far more interesting.

I considered how gray whales often travel alone or in unstable groups. How, after impregnating a fertile cow, the male whale will abandon the female and her offspring. How long-term bonds between individual gray whales are observed to be extremely rare.

There was something about these magnificent creatures that seemed so lonely, swimming in the vastness of the ocean without the camaraderie of kin. I saw that there was value in the freedom that kind of lifestyle afforded, but there was also a potential for an acute longing that seemed unbearable even for the most independent among us.

9
When the Discontented Disappear

I met Eric at a campground during my time in the Everglades. The other leaders and I had just finished our ten-day Wilderness Waterway excursion. Our clients had gone home, and we were busy cleaning and organizing gear when, out of nowhere, a lanky, tanned, handsome man strode into the campground. His unassuming swagger and scrappy-looking demeanor made me perk up. From his outdoorsy appearance, I would *never* have guessed that he was a New York City native. Now, he was getting used to a different kind of wilderness away from the urban jungle.

We hit it off, and I learned that he advocated for recycling programs, ran his own moving company, and lived in a rat-infested apartment on the Lower East Side where the toilet of the heroin-addicted upstairs neighbors leaked brown through the ceiling. Eric was quick to anger, and often badgered people for littering, screaming in people's faces. Scrappy, indeed. By the time he was sixteen, Eric had already been arrested for protesting nuclear power plants. As Eric's half-brother, Christopher Ketcham, wrote in 'The End of the (Green)

River' for *Men's Journal*, 'Although he loved New York, [Eric] hated that it was the epicenter of the materialism and bloated self-regard that he thought in the end would destroy the planet.'

Since it was the end of our excursion, I was invited to party with my fellow trip leaders that night, but after meeting Eric—this man who seemed so interesting—I decided I just wanted to keep talking. That evening, we went to the grocery store and bought dinner fixings. Back at our campsite, we told adventure stories. Eric mainly shared stories focused on kayaking and water sports. I told him about climbing and hiking routes. We would have loved to sleep outside under a blanket of stars, but that was *not* an option as the mosquitoes were so thick that we could kill a dozen with one swat against an arm, and the incessant buzzing in our ears would drive even the sanest person mad. So, in the tent we remained. We did not sleep that night, but we felt bonded to each other by morning.

Eric was visiting the Everglades so he could meet with his father, a fashion industry executive. I learned that Eric navigated a complicated relationship with the material world. He was uncomfortable with his privilege, identifying more as a Christopher McCandless type, someone who would choose simplicity over abundance, adventure over comfort.

Eric and I spent a day in Key West shopping for a bathing suit for a boat trip with his father. Eric waited outside the fitting room while I tried on numerous bikinis, modeling each of them for him. Normally, I would have been shy in a situation like this, since, thinking of myself first and foremost as a naturalist, I had never given much thought to my appearance. However, fresh off the paddling trip in the Everglades, with my upper body sculpted, I noticed myself observing my reflection in the mirror, admiring it. I had been lifting canoes and hauling gear, paddling long distances. I noticed Eric checking me out, too, and he gladly offered his expert opinions on the bathing suits, and I decided that the apple did not appear to have fallen far from the fashion designer father's tree. I picked out a couple of cute suits and we headed to the marina.

Eric did not love his father's boat, which was a bulky, showy yacht. He preferred sailboats instead, and this boat had no sail and was rocky on the waves, sitting high on the ocean, swaying and heaving. The choppy seas made me start to feel sick, so I jumped into the clear blue water to find balance. Eric followed, and we swam among the manta rays and schools of shimmering fish. When we clambered back onto the boat, Eric's father wanted to show us the custom-made curtains and matching shirts that he raved about.

For me, our time spent on the yacht was a brief glimpse into a surreal world of wealth. For Eric, though, it was a reality he was constantly trying to escape. While on the yacht, he grew irritable, and I guessed he was simply having re-entry issues, given that he had just finished a three-week solo kayaking expedition through the Everglades, during which he had been chased by alligators, but had not seen a single other human soul. However, it was not just that he wanted to get as far away from that boat as possible. He was strong and smart, and he could also be intense and opiniated. He wanted to save the world, one recyclable at a time. He was a man who defied definition and would not fit into any sort of box. As much as he extolled the virtues of the anti-materialist, Earth-protector lifestyle, he did not want to be called a hippie, resentful of the stereotypes that came with the subculture. Neither did he want to associate himself with the 'preppies' of New York. At heart, he was a loner, and as much as I was intrigued by him, respected his values and admired his passion, we eventually parted ways.

In Krakauer's book, *Into the Wild*, he describes how a young man from a well-to-do family named Christopher McCandless grew restless within the confines of capitalism, so he relinquished his inheritance and hitchhiked to Alaska, where he walked alone into the wilderness. There, north of Denali National Park, he lost his life, the cause of death presumably starvation, complicated by toxic plants.

Long after Eric and I dated, I received an unexpected letter from Eric's mother in which she described that it was one of the hardest letters that she had ever had to write. She explained that she had found my letters to Eric, and had known that we were close. She wanted to let me know that Eric's red kayak and his body had been found off the coast of Oregon. She was destroyed by grief, but she wanted me to know that he had been living the life he dreamed of and one that he had made for himself.

In 1989, Eric had written a mock will, where he had specified that he wanted his tens of thousands of dollars of savings (a product of his thriftiness) to go to the Rocky Mountain Institute, an organization dedicated to research in the general field of sustainability.

A couple of years later, Eric had traveled from New York City to the West where he had attended an outdoor adventure school and trained in rafting, guiding, and wilderness first aid so he could become a whitewater guide. He had become adept at boating and the instructors were impressed by his skill. Eric had been so flattered that he had phoned his mother to tell her the news. To celebrate, he headed to Coos Bay off the Oregon coast to kayak the spot where two rivers funnel into the bay, which can create roiling conditions that are tricky for even the most skilled boaters. On June 12, 1991, around four p.m., Eric paddled his kayak into the surf. That day, four people—including Eric—drowned. The wild, frigid waters off the Oregon Coast had stolen Eric.

Eric's close friends and family would have agreed that he was a troubled, tortured soul at times. He wanted the world to be a certain way, for people to care deeply for the environment, and it often did not turn out that way. Now, Eric was finally at peace.

Still, I continued to be unsettled by Eric's sad exit from this world. It sent a shiver down my spine the same way Christopher McCandless's story did. How the impulse to disengage with society could have such dire consequences. It reminded me how I needed both nature and people to feel whole. As much as I was always searching for peace in the wilderness, I was also always searching for deeper, sustained connection with the people in my life.

10
The Shadow of Loss in a Bright Time

The warm glow of hindsight has turned my five years as a park educator in Yosemite into a dreamy stretch of time in my life. My colleagues and I did our best to teach kids that 'nature is cool'. Since teaching is a good way to learn, we taught the kids to teach other kids. We played a game called 'Each One, Teach One', where the students took turns explaining interesting facts about nature to their classmates as we walked and talked along a trail. I delighted in watching our students lean in and study the puzzle-piece tapestry of ponderosa pine bark, or to hear their questions about animals that lived in the park, to watch their intrepid young selves withstand sleet, rain, and snow to learn about the natural world.

In my memory, when we weren't working, my colleagues and I frolicked in the meadows, played music among the pines, hikes and climbed. There, we lived in a bubble. We had immediate community, minimal stress, a low cost of living, and unlimited opportunities for outdoor recreation and get-togethers. It was a place where, most of the time, I felt safe, nurtured, and loved.

Each day, after teaching, I would take some time to sit along Crane Creek and watch the riffles go by. I often meditated on the reflections cast into the water by the snow plant, the manzanita, and ferns in the pools that gathered in the eddies. There, I would contemplate life's mysteries, slipping outside my body and sitting in quiet introspection. Sometimes, I would surface from this centered place and chuckle, considering my East Coast Catholic girl upbringing and wondering how I had gotten here.

Because we lived in the great outdoors in an adventurous community, it was also a place where a climbing accident or outdoor mishap could bend our world to its snapping point. Injury and death can more easily find those who push the limits, so our adventurous community was no stranger to loss. There was one accident, however, which, due to my involvement, shook me to my core.

One warm day, a climbing partner and I grabbed a friend's dog and made for Crane Creek, rock-hopping along our route, enjoying the sun on our skin and the cool breeze created from the rush of nearby water.

At one point, the dog wandered ahead of us and, before I could stop him, trotted to the edge of the roaring Crane Creek waterfall. Screaming, I ran toward him. "Come back! Come back!" I yelled.

Approaching him, I tripped and slid over smooth river rock, thinking for a moment that I would go over the edge myself. My friend scrambled after us, but it was too late. The dog slipped over the edge of the waterfall, his small paws clawing at the polished granite and slippery green algae, not finding purchase. I flung myself as close to the edge as I could, but I was powerless to prevent the dog's fate; I wasn't going to bring him back from over the precipice.

We ran down the side of the cliff to the bottom of the waterfall. "Please, do something!" I screamed at my friend. "Help him!"

I could tell he was not keen on recovering what he could only assume was a dead body, but I implored him once more. "Please, help," I begged, collapsing onto the ground.

Finally, my friend checked the water and found the dog floating in the pool beneath the waterfall. He brought the body near shore. I cowered.

"There is nothing we can do," he said. "He's gone."

I felt nauseous, dizzy. Guilt sank into me, making me feel leaden. Slowly, we hiked up Crane Flat Road to my home. On the way, my friend did his best to comfort me, but his efforts were useless; I was devastated.

Feeling too terrified to tell the dog's owner, I asked my friend to break the news.

Later, once I had gained some courage, I wrote a letter filled with regret and remorse and left the note on the owner's doorstep during a time he wouldn't be there. I knew I was being cowardly, but I could not bear to face him. The tragedy was still too fresh and surreal.

I returned to his house four days later, crawling to his doorstep weeping. When he came to the door, I cried even harder. "I'm sorry. I'm so, so sorry," I said between sobs.

Gently, he calmed me down. "It wasn't your fault," he said. "That dog was a crazy pup. We have been through lots of adventures together. I took him down dangerous rapids all over these mountains and he always stood on the front tube of the raft."

I pictured the dog peering over the edge of the raft into the rapids, and the thought brought me some small amount of relief.

A month before this, my friend had shown me photos of his trip to Nepal. Now, he explained how he had applied some of the Buddhist precepts he had learned in his travels to the passing of his dog, how he had held the body in his arms for a time, saying goodbye to his soul, setting him free and letting him pass gently to the other side. Then, he had gone to the Foresta Meadow and buried the dog there in a shallow grave, hoping the coyotes might make good use of his body, returning him to the earth.

While his kind assurances helped to bring me some peace about the tragic incident, I still never forgave myself. It became the reason I decided I would never have a dog of my own, since there would always be the possibility of loss hanging over that relationship. It took about ten years to summon the courage and wherewithal to be ready and able to think about getting a puppy—a sweet, yellow Labrador Retriever named Joss. I wanted desperately to have that unconditional love and constant responsibility in my life. It was great practice in being dependable and having an animal be reliant upon me, ultimately teaching me that I could be a safe and fun dog owner.

Years later, I would feel the pull of wanting to build a family. It was such a strong, deep desire that I had to face any fears of loss head on, forcing myself to practice active gratitude for the time I have with those I love most. In the end, being a parent has been the most challenging and rewarding gift I have ever experienced.

11
When There's No Meaning to be Made

Ten years after my road trip with Feather, long after we had parted ways, I was on an eight-hour train ride from Anchorage to Denali National Park when a woman tapped me on the shoulder.

"Do you remember me?" she asked. "Weren't you in my home years ago with Feather? He was my friend."

I looked at her in disbelief, vaguely recognizing her face. Then it all came flooding back to me—her hospitality when she had graciously hosted me and Feather in her Los Angeles home during our road trip. She had made dinner and offered us a hot shower. Now, she looked at me with grief in her eyes.

"Are you here for Feather's memorial?" she asked.

"No…" I said, my chest constricting. Tentatively, I asked, "What happened to Feather?"

"He passed away recently."

I pressed the woman for more details. "What happened to sweet Feather?" I asked, tears welling in my eyes.

The muscles in her face tensed, and she looked strained. She told me Feather had been murdered. "There was a call from a guy who needed something dropped off way out in the bush," she sputtered. "Feather flew in and landed on the dirt strip, and before he could even step off the plane, the man came out of his home, shot Feather, and killed him."

I covered my mouth with a hand and squeezed my eyes shut.

"The guy claimed he had been startled, but he was the one who had called for the flight. None of it makes any sense."

I learned that the memorial was happening that weekend and that our train would be passing through the location where it would be held. Feather had been cremated and his ashes would be honored by his family, friends, past partners, and neighbors. Rocked by shock, I felt an urge to jump off the train, run to where his ashes were, and to say goodbye, wanting to feel connected to the other mourners who would be celebrating him, to see his ashes spread around. Either that, or I wanted to take some of his ashes to spread in the Grand Canyon, where it all began for us. I wanted to give his mom and dad a hug and tell them how sorry I was that they had lost their beloved son. But, as the train chugged past Feather's home and community, I stayed on the train, glued there by some ineffable force that was instructing me to move forward instead of retreating to the past.

***

My time in Alaska was bruised by grief. I tried out my new position working for a fly-in ecolodge, but it was not a good fit. It had been a hunting lodge operation and the energy of the whole scene was off, not to mention some glaring safety issues. I chalked it up to a poor choice for employment and said that I would make a better choice next time. Meanwhile, I was sifting through my sadness over Feather, as if I were dipping a hand over and over into glacial runoff, hoping that when I lifted my hand from the silted water, it would be crystal clear. Each time, though, my palm was filled with debris.

The main reason I had wanted to come to Alaska was because it had been the place my dad had longed to go his whole life, always telling my mother that one day, he would visit. But his untimely death at thirty-nine prevented his dream from coming true. I thought by going there myself I could bring him with me in spirit. When I stepped off the Alaska Railroad at the Denali train station and settled into national park life, I could feel my dad in the tundra, rivers, and under the northern lights. I looked forward to sharing this magical place with him. However, Alaska is a place without rules. It is big and beastly, with real threats of danger all around. Although I had done quite a bit of solo backpacking in the Grand Canyon and Zion National Park, I was not accustomed to being on the lookout for grizzlies, wolverines, and moose. Here, bears seemed as big as trucks, with teeth and claws that could rip a human apart with seemingly minimal effort. In the remote part of the park, grizzly bears were not accustomed to encounters with humans, so their confusion and fear could lead them to unpredictable behavior. Wolverines, though rarely seen, are territorial, muscular scavengers, capable of tearing into frozen bone. Moose can be aggressive if disturbed, and, weighing at least fourteen hundred pounds, make for a formidable opponent when they decide to charge and trample a potential threat. It did not help my fears that out here the landscape was so vast and empty and unpopulated that any cries for help would be swallowed by all that space.

In addition to the adapting to a new place, I was also trying to bend my life around my new boyfriend, Dylan. That summer, I struggled not to cling to him for comfort and support.

Before Alaska, I had thought that being fatherless had made me fearless. My whole life since my father's death, I had faced the world head-on, leaping into adventure, forging my own path. Now, grieving the losses of both Feather and my father, and trying to maintain my independence and self-reliance within my new relationship, I felt adrift and afraid. It felt as if, after years of distracting myself with dogged self-determination—always on the move, always moving forward—I was now having to sit still long enough that the loneliness was finding me in this wide, open, raw expanse. No matter how much I tried avoiding my own sadness, that season felt like a time of unreconcilable loss.

At the end of the summer, I left Alaska, unsure whether I could endure a dark, hard winter there. I would return, though, wanting to give Alaska a second chance, and hoping that the next time, I could honor my father the way I had originally intended. Instead of the dark seep of sadness, I wanted to experience the bright spots this powerful place could offer. This time, I took a position as Park Service Ranger naturalist in Denali National Park. This time, I wove through the Alaskan tussocks, clumps of grass in the subarctic tundra. I observed black spruce, quaking aspen, and paper birch, three of only eight tree species found within the boundaries of the park. I gazed in awe at the Aurora Borealis lighting up the sky.

That year, Dylan and I worked together, and we explored the Alaskan wilds via an enormous trailless wilderness, sharing unforgettable experiences.

One day, as we lounged on a ground cloth in the tundra and soaked up the long summer rays, a couple of young grizzlies came into view and cavorted around with each other near a small herd of caribou. I was transfixed, watching these two species co-mingle in such proximity, minding their own business. Eventually, the bear cubs approached us, their heads swaying, their noses smelling the air for information.

Then, they charged at us. Dylan leapt up and grabbed the silver ground cloth, shaking it to scare the grizzlies away. They turned, realizing we were not a typical food source and were not there to harm them. Soon, they were ignoring us again, along with the caribous, which continued munching on nearby grasses and sedges. Although we were unscathed, we were both shaken. However, even though my heart was pounding, I felt safe. By facing my fear and returning to Alaska, I had reclaimed a part of myself that I had been missing during my first visit. It was not fearlessness. Instead, it was something more akin to a willingness to lean into my fear, reminding myself that it was okay to feel afraid. The world could be a frightening place, especially while moving through it as a woman without a father. But I was learning that I could be both afraid and safe. Nature could pose threats while also providing peace. By confronting that which made me most afraid—sorrow, loss, abandonment—I could begin to heal. I just had to allow myself to be open to the healing balm that wild spaces can offer. Even in the midst of my suffering, I could find deep connection with the natural world. I could have encounters with wildlife that would unfold my heart. I could begin to imagine what seeing this place through my father's eyes might have felt like—to finally fulfill a lifelong yearning. The feeling was tantamount to falling in love.

***

A few years after Feather's death, I called his mother. We shared stories and listened to each other try to articulate the ways in which Feather had impacted our lives. I recounted our visit to see them during our road trip, and I told his mother that she had raised an extraordinary, enigmatic, charismatic young man. My heart was breaking for her as we spoke, and I could hear the devastation in her voice, her life still so clearly shattered by loss. But it felt good to share this loss and to feel connected to Feather through her. Speaking to her now, I felt that I wasn't leaning backward to try to secure something that was no longer within arm's reach. Instead, this was a way to move forward, to heal, to commune, and to honor.

Twenty years after Feather's murder, I drove a Volkswagen bus along the same stretch of highway through Big Sur that Feather and I had traveled during our road trip. I had not cried for him in some time, but seeing the Pacific Ocean sparkling—the same ocean that Feather had introduced me to—I began to weep. Several months prior, my mother had passed away peacefully in her sleep, which was the type of passing that she had prayed for through much of her later life. I grieved her loss and continued to miss her presence every day, but her death felt like an acceptable reality—one that I had seen coming for a while. My mother had lived a long, full, beautiful life. She had accomplished what she had set out to achieve, and had experienced wonders, contentment, and love. Although I had not been ready to lose her, I believe that she had been ready to go. She crossed over at the age of eighty-nine.

Feather's death, and my father's as well, were too abrupt to make any sense of. My father's death had seemed unfair because I had been so young, and his life has been cut much too short. Feather's violent death had seemed unfair because he had been much too young and the manner of his passing had been tragic. To be killed by such a horrific act left a stain on his life that I was still trying to get out. He had been ripped from the world before his time had come. Dying due to medical, accidental, or natural causes seemed more acceptable, somehow. Even Eric's death had made more sense to me. Or, at least, I had felt more peace with his disappearance, knowing that his beautiful soul was now at peace. I liked to believe he was watching over me. I even talked to him frequently while hiking or boating, feeling his presence and guidance, believing he kept me safe during adventures, even if I was just driving along a highway like I was now. I could not ignore, however, how two men I had loved had passed away so tragically. Why had two incredible human beings been taken from this Earth much too soon? I knew that both men had been adventure-seeking, risk-taking men with strong minds of their own. The fact that Feather's life had been taken had left me feeling—even twenty years later—muddled and unmoored.

There had been two other deaths in my life that had impacted me similarly to Feather's. During my training week at Zion National Park, my roommate, Emily, and I were called to respond to a hiker who had fallen off the Angel's Landing trail. We were young, eager first responders—ready to help. We quickly ascended the trail, cruising up the switchback section of trail as fast as we could and then made our way down to where the injured woman had landed, from many feet above. Emily checked her vitals and immediately began compressions and breaths. The woman's abdomen was distended, leading us to believe that she was suffering from internal injuries. Her vitals were weak, and they continued to drop. It was a stormy day, and as we struggled to keep her alive, rainbows stretched across the sky. Ravens cawed and swooped down over us. Despite our efforts, we lost her. As we tried to regain our composure, sunbeams reached down through the black clouds.

The strangest part of the experience was that the woman's hiking companion had seemed nonchalant about the incident. He had claimed that the woman had slipped while hiking, which had left me feeling unsettled. Years later, I would learn that the woman's family believed that he had pushed her to her death, after he had bumped up her life insurance.

The other grim tragedy that overlapped with my career was the brutal, fatal attack of a fellow educator in Yosemite National Park. She had been a victim in a series of murders that had rocked our close-knit community. I learned of the heinous crime while on my honeymoon in Africa after climbing Kilimanjaro.

During my travels to Kenya, Tanzania and Zimbabwe, I grabbed whatever bit of reading material and news I could in a place bereft of available literature. I picked up a news magazine and read what I could not believe to be true. It felt so far away, yet it also felt so personal. Like many in our tribe of Yosemite locals, I thought: that could have been me. Although I was traveling in Africa at the time of her murder, I was left feeling rattled. I can only imagine that the feeling was akin to a service man or woman—such as a paramedic, peace officer, or military personnel—losing one of their own. We educators felt this one as a collective assault on our community.

Like with Feather's murder, there was no rhyme or reason to these deaths. No way to make sense of them. My whole life, no matter how much I have tried to extract meaning or locate some life lesson, I have come up short, which, I suppose, is its own kind of lesson.

12
Breaking Open

Eventually, after three healthy, meaningful, three-year relationships and several dates in between, I would meet the man who I would marry and raise children with. I would meet someone for whom I would be willing to give up some of my independence, who was also someone who valued that independence in me. But first, I'd had to meet and partner with various others with whom I needed to learn lessons about the world, about relationships and—most importantly—about myself. Through each relationship, I was able to see myself a bit more clearly, and to envision a life that could be shared, but that would still be unequivocally mine.

After my time in Yosemite, I was getting the itch to settle down and store all my belongings in one place. I had grown tired of moving from park to park, state to state. I wanted to simply 'be' for a little while. I began dating a man named Ryan after we met at the Strawberry Bluegrass Festival in Yosemite, near the Hetch Hetchy Reservoir. It was an open-air festival attended by thousands of frolicking, dancing, bluegrass-loving folks who gathered together for a long weekend of music in the woods. The songs drifted through the mountain air, and it seemed as though we were all floating along with them.

Ryan asked for my phone number, and we started talking. He lived in San Jose, teaching at a private school after graduating from Stanford University with a degree in marine biology. I was still working as an environmental educator in Yosemite National Park. We hit it off and decided to see each other more. He would come to the park, and we would take long walks and talk about everything from Buddhism to classical music.

Eventually, my guard fell and I found myself falling hard for Ryan. Then, we decided to work enough to save money to travel for seven months, which we did. He finished out his school year and gave notice, and I worked at random jobs that included catering at high-end Silicon Valley parties and working at health food stores. In Palo Alto California, I worked for Steve Jobs's estate, and once swam naked in Jobs's pool, unaware who Steve Jobs was at the time. All I had known from the estate caretakers was that the homeowner liked bing cherries, avocados, long walks, and beautiful gardens.

In the autumn of 1990, Ryan and I flew to Nepal and spent three months trekking in the Himalayas. We did a ten-day vipassana meditation retreat where we sat cross-legged for up to eight hours a day, legs falling asleep and tingling. We ate vegetarian meals every day, slept separately—men in their dorm, women in theirs. A little stir-crazy from all the sitting meditation, I would walk in a circle during my walking meditation in the garden and nearly dug a path in the dusty soil with my sandal-footed, repetitive steps.

One day, I walked behind a building and saw a whole litter of puppies. I played with them—even talked to them, despite it being a silent meditation. I needed connection and communication, even if it was with canines. By day seven, Ryan and I were restless and itching to continue with our adventures.

Two days later, we were on the Sunkosi River with a group of people and some adventurous guides. After a week of silent meditation, the transition was jarring. The outfitter's owner was from Australia, and as we quickly learned, had a wild streak. Under his watch, kayakers were flipping in their boats and swimming wild rapids. Meanwhile, some guests experimented with local mushrooms and weed. A female passenger, who happened to be an accountant, underwent a drastic personality change over the course of ten hours, going from being overly talkative, controlling, and intense to silent, withdrawn, and bedraggled. I was concerned and kept an eye out for her welfare, hoping that she would recover quickly and get back to her old self—if maybe just a little more relaxed. Somehow, we all survived the trip.

Next, Ryan and I trekked to the Thame monastery and sat with monks, giving offerings and leaning into the present moment. We both relished the peace and quietude, but I noticed that Ryan seemed interested to the point of wanting to completely devote himself to a monastic lifestyle and the practice of meditation.

"I could see myself just staying here, sitting, meditating, eating simply, chanting, and living peacefully with the monks," he said.

As much as I understood where he was coming from, it hurt my feelings to hear him imagining a life that didn't seem to include me. I tried to understand and wanted him to do whatever made him feel fulfilled and happy, but my ego was still bruised.

***

It took me until I was twenty-seven years old to begin to process my feelings around losing my father so young. I had done enough counseling and had studied enough psychology in college to recognize that I still had unfinished business.

During a trip to Wyoming and Montana with Ryan, I experienced a transformative moment that felt as though I was starting the process of tackling my unfinished business. We were hiking in high alpine meadows lined with carpets of colorful wildflowers on a sunny blue-sky day. Maybe it had been something about that wide open sky that led me to an openness of heart that allowed me to access deeper feelings. My feelings simmered, then bubbled up, then burst out and poured out of me. Ryan had hiked on ahead of me to the next ridge, so I lay in the meadow and looked up at the vast sky above. I screamed and cried out at the top of my lungs.

"I'm sorry, Dad, I'm sorry!" I yelled. "I'm so sorry that you died of a horrible disease! I'm sorry for being angry at you for leaving us. I forgive you and I forgive myself for being mad at you; a six-year-old does not understand death. I love you and I'm sorry," I screamed into the wilderness. For so long, I had carried an unconscious anger toward my father for abandoning me, even though it had not been his choice. As a young family, we had not talked about his six-month lung cancer illness, death, or our feelings around it. My time in the meadow was a turning point of accepting his death for what it was: a sad, unfortunate loss, instead of intentional abandonment. This realization marked the beginning of my healing, though I still had a lot of work to do.

***

One night, during our time in Palo Alto, in the middle of a deep sleep, I had a dream that felt so real that I woke up with tears streaming down my face. In the dream, I had felt as if my whole chest had been cracked open like an egg, exposing my fragile, beating heart. I had known immediately upon waking that the dream had signified that I was having trouble opening my heart to Ryan, allowing him into my world and trusting that he wouldn't leave me or abandon me. I went into the small bathroom next to our room, where I could sob and shake in private. But Ryan was intuitive, patient, and aware, and sensed what was going on.

"Betty Ann, come back to bed, please," he implored gently. "Be with me now, and trust in this."

Ryan had consistently shown me through his actions that he was a solid, trustworthy, kind, and caring man. I was beside myself that, even with all his reassurances, I still could not seem to open myself up and let him fully in.

"I'm not coming in after you," Ryan said. "You need to come out here on your own."

It took fifteen minutes, but I finally made my way back to him, crawling on my hands and knees to our futon and into his arms. We didn't say anything; Ryan simply held me while I sobbed in his warm embrace and tried to feel the force of his love, hoping that maybe his love would be enough to reassure me that it was safe to trust.

Ryan's tender heart and unconditional love helped to melt that shell from around my heart. That night, I had felt a sacred and blessed healing, one that was the beginning of my letting go and learning to let love in. After we had broken up, he wrote me a long letter, explaining that he hoped that the scared little girl would continue to grow up and learn to trust. Eventually, I would. And it was because of Ryan that I began to do just that.

***

I lived with Dylan for three years on and off, part of that time spent in Alaska, and eventually in Vail, Colorado, where I worked at a jewelry store, taught Nordic skiing, and got a job at the hospital as a unit intake person in the emergency department. Meanwhile, Dylan was a part-time resident of Vail, guiding backcountry ski tours during the winter season.

Dylan and I summited Mount Rainier in Washington state together, just a few weeks after we had met, climbing to fourteen thousand, four hundred and eleven feet, feeling humbled by the rigorous activity, and how it so thoroughly wreaks havoc on the brain and body. Dylan was a climbing ranger on Mount Rainier and a senior guide in the backcountry around Vail and Aspen. He had a great deal of experience guiding people through avalanche-prone country and teaching them avalanche safety and backcountry skills. Dylan was just as skilled at having a great time, cracking jokes, and telling tales. He was witty, sarcastic, with an almost cynical type of Midwestern humor that was often lost on me, but was appreciated by many of his clients.

It was hard maintaining a relationship with Dylan because he was always off guiding a trip and leaving me back home in Vail. When we worked in remote Alaska, he had several frightening encounters with bears in the backcountry, never certain whether their curiosity with him were mock charges or actual attempted attacks. Far away from civilization, with minimal gear and medical supplies and no means for communication, these experiences left him rattled. He would come home like a deer in the headlights, almost seeming to suffer symptoms aligned with post-traumatic stress disorder.

Back at home in Vail, I felt lonely and unsure when Dylan took his trips. There were small moments when I doubted the success of our union. We enjoyed wonderful adventures together, yet in the larger landscape of our relationship, it seemed that trust and commitment were missing from our connection. I was finally opening my heart to a relationship, but Dylan was not meeting me there when it mattered. With each disappointment, I felt deflated and crushed. We had given it our best effort. We were even calling ourselves 'pre-engaged', at one point.

"You're either engaged or you're not," my friends would say.

We had summited Rainier, scaled peaks in Colorado, had traveled around the state, and now were living together, yet I knew it was not enough to sustain a long-term committed relationship.

It was through Dylan, though, that I would meet the man of my dreams: someone who cries during sentimental movies, who is kind and compassionate, and who walks this Earth with his head held high. He would be the one who would become my husband, with whom I would raise two remarkable boys.

Dylan ended up moving to Alaska, working trail crews, doing natural resource management for Denali

National Park, working as an excellent environmental steward, and hanging out with sled dogs. Even though we didn't work out as a couple, he has always had my admiration, and I remain proud to call him a friend.

***

As for my own journey, I took my time getting to know Chip while we both worked in the Vail hospital, he as an emergency department physician and I as an intake clerk, after renewing my emergency medical technician certification. We had worked together for about six months, both focused at work and busy during our time off.

After ski season ended, I spent time in Boulder working numerous outdoor jobs, with the highlight of my guiding career being taking a group of twelve high school students on a six-week immersion course in the Annapurna region of Nepal. The students lived with local families, learning about their culture, language, religion, and art—an experience full of adventure and the challenges of being in a developing country. We participated in hard manual labor, building a wooden bridge over a raging creek. We climbed over beautiful mountain passes, watched the stars from the rooftops of the family teahouses, and bonded as a group.

When I returned from Nepal, I was feeling ready to settle down more than ever. I was living back in Boulder, but was restless and unsure of my path moving forward.

One night, I sat straight up in my bed, setting my intentions: 'I'm open and ready for someone in my life that is ready for commitment, has integrity and stability, and wants the same things in life.'

The very next day, I got a phone call from a nurse friend who had also worked with Chip. She said that he had asked her for my contact information, and she said she would ask me first if I wanted to share it with him. *Of course* I wanted to speak with him! The next day, Chip called asking for a date. We went out for a delicious dinner, hiked through Chautauqua Park, and then we kissed. Chip said, "It would be great if you would come up to the mountains and spend Christmas with me." I did, and we enjoyed a magical few days telemark skiing and sharing long, wintery hikes in the woods.

Later that month, I got my own place in the mountains, though we stayed mostly inseparable. Being a decisive sort of man, he was certain of things between us, because two months later he said, "I want to get to know you for a year, then I want you to be my wife." He proposed on the mountain the following Christmas on a crisp, clear Colorado bluebird morning.

Finally, the walls around my heart came crashing down. Over my years with Chip, I have learned to trust, nurturing that little girl inside me who was scared, hurt, and abandoned. I'd felt like I'd had to do it all on my own. Chip showed me that it was okay to receive help. Before him, I had not been fully able to trust fully or to relinquish control. It took me time to let my guard down, but when I finally did, I learned that I could be independent yet connected, strong yet vulnerable. I learned I could be whole.

It has been a long journey, and there is still farther to go down the path of self-acceptance and growth. Learning to love has been a journey that has cracked open the outer shell of my heart and has revealed an open, trusting soul. In the end, it was never about the guys; it was about the experiences that came along with them. Each one of them showed me a different part of myself. They were my teachers, and I will forever feel grateful for their lessons. In any relationship, there is what happens between the couple, then there is the person's private life. But there is also a third factor: one's inner being. In order for a relationship to work, all three have to be in harmony. A relationship can't work if a couple isn't getting enough alone time, or too much. A relationship also isn't going to work if there's an equal balance of couple time and alone time, but one or both people in the relationship aren't staying true to their inner selves. I had needed to find myself before I could give myself fully, so that I could recognize whether my inner being was still in balance within the dynamics of partnership. I feel lucky to have found someone who lets me be exactly who I need to be.

Part IV
Art and Beauty

13
Made with Love

My first sweetheart, Tate, who I met in high school art class, was half Iroquois. His father was full-blooded Native American from the Mohawk Nation. We fell madly in love, and while he fished along the creeks, I wandered through meadows looking at wildflowers and lay in the tall grasses looking up at the passing clouds. With me, Tate shared his fierce pride for his culture, unapologetically explaining to me their belief systems, their reverence for life, their respect for Mother Earth and Father Sky. Tate took me to visit longhouses on the Onondaga Reservation where he knew some of the families who were celebrating the autumn corn harvest with ritual and dance.

Tate and his father made me a deerskin dress from a buck that his father had shot with a bow and arrow. He had tanned the hide and the texture was soft as a baby's bottom. I wore it several times throughout our time together. It was a piece of such beauty and I felt proud to wear such a special garment.

Tate was a much better artist than I, making seed bead belts on a bead loom, weaving textiles, crafting leather belts and pouches, and molding pottery in the art studio of our beloved art teacher, Barry.

In class, Tate and I admired Barry's nurturing demeanor and the way he gently guided us through lessons on art and life. We appreciated the creative space and did our bestto make good use of our time in class. My love for Barry and my fellow students made the class feel like family. There, I felt safe and respected, not pushed to do anything that didn't feel authentic.

Most of all, I admired Barry for his willingness to be firm when he needed to be. He would remind us to respect the clay, because after all, he was a 'mudman': a master potter.

One day, I made a misshapen, crude beer mug with the word '*Lowenbrau*' ('lion's brew') etched into the surface of some beautiful, marbled porcelain and gray clay mixture that had been painstakingly mixed and cured. Barry took one look at my 'art' and scoffed.

"Oh, really?" he said. "That's what you made out of that beautiful clay?"

I began to feel ashamed, then Barry smiled and said, "I think you can do better than that." I respected him even more after that, for he held us to high expectations—the sign of a good teacher.

In a way, Barry was a role model to me, someone whom I considered to be a mentor and friend. He was kind, caring, and inspirational in the way that he sought to be an example for us. He was a hardworking, dedicated teacher who showed up for his students every day. More than anything else, though, he was the person who showed me what beauty can be—that beauty does not just reside in the final form of an object, but that it has a lot to do with *how* the object is made. How, sometimes, an object's beauty can be directly proportional to the amount of love that is poured into it, like the deerskin dress that Tate and his dad had made for me. The dress was a beautiful object, sure. But its beauty was also wrapped up in the love with which Tate had constructed it, the care his father had taken to kill the buck, honor its life, and carefully tan the hide; the love he felt for his son, and the love his son felt for me. In essence, Barry taught me that beauty, at its very core, is made from love.

***

In my late twenties, I attended an Insight workshop, a self-growth and awareness seminar. For the 'stretch' session during the commencement ceremony, the participants were asked to trade garments with one another. The goal of the exercise was to step out of one's normal shoes, to push ourselves past our regular boundaries and to try something different.

I traded garments with a gorgeous, elegant southern belle who had brought a white 'coming out' debutante gown to the seminar. I had brought the deerskin dress that Tate's father had made for me. The stunning debutante wore the soft, supple deerskin. Meanwhile, I stepped into the crisp, pure white gown. I danced to Carole King's 'Beautiful'. The debutante chose an earthy drumbeat for her background music. She moved her body in ethereal movements, grounded to the earth in a spiritual aliveness. During my 'stretch', I began spinning around and around with abandonment and joy, feeling like Daddy's little princess during her coming out debutante ball, during which her father would have proudly given her away for her first dance with a boy, and she would have come of age with the blessing of her father under his watchful, protective eye. What a dream it was, to imagine this alternate reality in which I still had a father. For just a few glorious moments, I felt his love and forgot that I had been abandoned so early in my life. My heart felt full and I could see how his love was there, even if he no longer was.

14
From Nest to Sky

After graduating from SUNY at Cortland with a bachelor's degree in biology and natural sciences, I felt as though I could identify nearly anything in the natural world—every tree, wildflower, bush, bird, and critter. I used this knowledge to land several positions at local nature education centers across Upstate New York. During one internship, I worked at Beaver Lake Nature Center with the Syracuse Zoo's collection of nearly ninety birds, mostly waterfowl. During nesting season, we helped with incubation work to increase the bird count.

One day, as I sloshed through the lake in waders toward the nest boxes, a black swan drifted up to me. I was startled by the nearness of this large bird with a six-foot wingspan, especially given that, if he had wanted to, he could have broken my arm or leg with one swift wing beat, and I wouldn't necessarily have been able to hold an attack on me against him, since I was the one who was flagrantly encroaching on the eggs that he was intent on guarding. Both male and female black swans are responsible for incubation duties and I appeared to be interrupting the male's shift. His eyes were red, which was a normal occurrence during breeding season (black swans' eyes turn from white to red during this time), but it gave him a more menacing look. Gently, I spoke to him, explaining that I meant no harm.

"Please don't hurt me," I murmured. "I come in peace to check your eggs. I know this looks suspicious, but I promise not to hurt you or your babies."

Whether due to trust or luck, the swan let me pass. I continued wading out through the green algae-strewn waters, listening to the cacophony of springtime mating season among the nearly one hundred captive birds, along with the wild birds that had come to join in the mesmerizing symphony.

When I reached the nest boxes, I checked them for eggs. If we found eggs, we were to carry them back to the incubators and replace them with 'dummy' eggs that the birds usually accepted and sat on. The natural eggs were placed in a more controlled environment where, we hoped, they would hatch successfully, without the risk of predators, weather changes, or other unpredictable threats. That spring, we hatched a gaggle of chicks from mandarin ducks (my personal favorite), pin-tailed ducks, mallards, green-winged teal, and—to our delight—a solitary black swan cygnet.

I felt maternal, almost, watching the waterfowl chicks use the pip tooth at the end of their beaks to crack the shell and make their way out into the world where they would eventually learn to fly, take to their wings, and view the Earth from above. It was extraordinary to think about how these little puffballs with beaks were born to fly, but first had to learn how to use the wings they had been given.

Both the male and female black swan parents raise their young for about nine months, at which point, it becomes time for their offspring to learn how to fly. How beautiful these creatures were, with their language of plaintive calls and parental pairings that were preserved for life. I found myself envious of the little cygnets with their protective fathers. I considered how I had fled the nest to spread my own wings and fly. But even though I had left home, I found beauty in the knowledge that a person could have more than one home in a life. For me, first it had been the safety of the nest, and now I was lucky enough to have found the freedom of the sky.

15
Open Your Eyes

Early in my career, before I became an official park ranger, I worked the fee collection station at the entrance for Zion National Park. As excited as I had been to be working within the national parks system, by the end of my time there, I began to feel some *Dirty Dancing*-style entitlement rising within me, though instead of 'Nobody puts Baby in the corner', it was 'Nobody puts Betty Ann in a box'. I kept hoping that one of the staff would transfer and I could step into a teaching position. I wanted to walk and talk, not sit in a hot, cramped shed handling people's money or tempering visitors' frustrations with having to pay to see one of the most beautiful places on Earth.

To avoid having to pay the entrance fee, a common remark was, "I'll just close my eyes as I drive through the park."

It grew tiring, feigning politeness and smiling each time someone tried to undervalue the service that I—and the National Park Service—were providing.

My hopes rose when a position opened up for another naturalist and I applied. However, a different woman got the job instead of me. From my young perspective, I assumed this would be my only window of opportunity to pursue the career of my dreams, and just as quickly as it had appeared, it had vanished. I could not fathom anyone wanting that position more than I did. I hiked along the Watchman Trail that wove through juniper, sage, and prickly pear cactus. I cried and stormed, raging at the seeming injustice of it all.

Rather than trying to convince people to pay to see the park, I wanted to make an argument for why the park was so beautiful. I wanted to take each of those resistant visitors by the hand and walk them through stands of mesquite and cliffrose, pointing out tiny pinyon mice darting from rock to rock, or the golden eagles perched on ponderosa snags, or mountain lion tracks imprinted in clay mud. I wanted to explain to them how water (or the lack thereof) is the determining factor in the desert. In the higher elevations, where rain and snowfall can reach an annual precipitation amount of up to twenty-six inches, greenleaf manzanita grow, and large mammals like elk, bear, and yellow-bellied marmots can be found. Descend to mid-elevation habitats, and you'll discover clusters of bigtooth maple and Utah juniper. Down in the desert, where annual precipitation can be as minimal as fifteen inches, desert tortoise and honey mesquite find their home. Near waterways, stands of cottonwoods, ash, and boxelder can be found lining the shorelines. Peer between fronds of maidenhair fern in spongy riparian hanging gardens, and you might find evidence of the rare Zion snail. Stay up past sunset and you might hear canyon treefrogs chirping.

I wanted to explain to visitors that it was because of the Zion-Mount Carmel highway that was completed in 1930 that they could even drive from Zion to Bryce, and that the highway remains one of the most impressive engineering feats in U.S. history. To finish the route, a five thousand, six hundred and thirteen-foot tunnel had to be added to compensate for the imposing sandstones cliffs in the park.

I wanted to warn hikers about the summer monsoons that send flash floods careening through canyons and filling up dry creek beds. The annual flooding, minimal arable land, and poor soil made it difficult for early settlers to take root here, and many communities abandoned certain settlements due to the relentless strain in such harsh conditions.

I also wanted visitors to this park to understand that indigenous people had been making a home here for centuries before the 1700s, when traders from New Mexico and fur trappers came on the scene, and then government surveyors added travel routes across the area. By 1872, as part of western surveys conducted by the U.S. Geological Survey, John Wesley Powell had explored areas surrounding Zion, and pack trails were soon well-worn by wagons making the journey from Santa Fe to California. Before all that, the area had been home to Southern Paiute who made the desert glow gold with plantings of sunflowers, corn, and squash. Other

Native communities traveled through the area seasonally, collecting seeds and nuts, and hunting game. Centuries before then, the Virgin Anasazi and the Parowan Fremont peoples had established gardens and year-round villages using grinding stones to process corn, an important staple. The Parowan Fremont even grew a drought- and cold-tolerant variety of corn that could survive at higher elevations. The Virgin Anasazi built homes on river terraces along what is now known as the Virgin River.

Yucca fiber sandals, baskets, nets, flaked stone knives, and dart points have been recovered from dry caves that are thought to have been made between 6000 B.C. and A.D. 500.

I wanted park visitors to see the park through my eyes, and I didn't think that was possible while I was sitting in a box. What I still had to learn, though, was that beauty was in the eye of the beholder. I could no more convince these strangers to love the park as much as I did as I could convince the park to hire me for the position I most wanted.

Between my jobs and travels over the years, when I would visit home, I would tell my mother how much fun I was having out West seeing all the national parks. "It's so beautiful and expansive in those wide, open spaces," I would tell her. "You would love it."

But, alas, she did not always love the road trips along steep, mountain ridges out West or anywhere. On a trip where I introduced her to Yosemite, I was reminded that my mother was deathly afraid of heights, and as my Aunt Betty drove over Tioga Pass above tree line, my mother cowered near the floor, terrified that the car, at any moment, might topple over a drop-off. Her fear was so huge that she could not enjoy the scenery.

"It's so scary and desolate," she said. "How come you like it here?"

It broke my heart to hear her say such things about a place that had stolen my heart. I told her that the mountains called to me. She still did not understand, but I was beginning to understand something about beauty and about those who choose to see it versus those who close their eyes. There was nothing wrong with people like my mother or Zion visitors who didn't appreciate all the wonders of that special place. They just didn't see what I saw. My vision had been strengthened by everything I'd read, everything I'd learned, and everything I'd remained curious about. It was as if my continued curiosity had given me rose-colored glasses, through which I could see a beauty that was shaped by my own excitement, making it distinctly, uniquely, more beautiful than I could ever possibly begin to explain.

Part V
Connection and Community

16
To Get Grounded, Go Home

After Feather picked me up at the end of my Colorado River rafting trip, we spent a few more days together before I caught a ride to Phoenix and flew to Oregon to begin my work as a firefighter at Crater Lake National Park. In some ways, I was relieved to once again be on my own as I got settled in my new work, without having to worry about anyone else's plans. I was proud to have secured a paid NPS position and did not want to be held back by the dreams and priorities of a male counterpart.

There were moments when I felt as though Feather was perfect for me, yet for whatever reason, I continued to struggle letting him fully into my heart.

Before I left, Feather had said, "I will get a vehicle somehow and come join you at Crater Lake."

"You do realize that I'll be busy training and working a lot, right?" I asked.

"Yes, darlin'," he said. "But I'm sure everything will work out. I just gotta be near you."

"I've worked hard in school for this break, and what I do for work is important. This is the next big adventure for me and I'm not going to mess it up by getting distracted by some gorgeous dude."

Before long, Feather had found an old Volkswagen bus and had fixed it up in his hometown. Once he got it running, he drove up to Crater Lake to join me.

While I worked hard to prove myself as the only woman on the crew, studying fire behavior and safety and trying my best to bond with my team while battling constant exhaustion, Feather used his charismatic charm to easily secure a position with the park concessionaire.

Feather and I were both too busy to relax much, but when we did, we went on long hikes, kissed in the woods, and returned to my tiny cubby hole of an attic loft that served as my home for the season. At five foot ten, I could barely stand upright under the low, slanted ceiling. At six feet tall, Feather had even more difficulty climbing up the narrow ladder and squeezing himself into the space. My park employee accommodations were dated, the product of either Work Projects Administration or Civilian Conservation Corps housing, which had been ambitious New Deal agencies that had employed over eight million people to carry out public works projects during the Great Depression. Decades later, our cabins—with their dry, thin walls, minimal insulation, and noisy floorboards—were now outmoded fire hazards (Crater Lake National Park and many other parks have since rebuilt ranger housing). Feather's employee housing wasn't much better. Although he occupied a small room on the top floor of the historic

Crater Lake Lodge, the space was bare bones and uninviting, and I never spent much time there.

At the end of a grueling fire season, Feather and I headed south to begin our road trip. Since I didn't know how to drive a stick shift and the vintage Volkswagen was finicky, Feather did all the driving. At first, I was fine being the navigator, but after days of travel, I began to grow restless, sensing that I was losing control of the direction in which I was steering my life. I did not want to stay in the passenger seat.

A rockhound, Feather wanted to stop at numerous rock shops along the way, combing through various collections of precious rocks and gems. He took me to meet his parents. He showed me the Pacific Ocean. Even though I was the keeper of the map, our destinations were dictated by Feather's wishes and whims.

We followed the whales south all the way to Mexico. My first time outside the United States, I was excited at first. But soon I realized, walking around Tijuana, that many eyes were on my naked legs, since I was wearing shorts in the blazing sun. I looked around and noticed that the local ladies had covered their legs with pants or long skirts. To avoid unsolicited attention, I quickly changed my wardrobe. I was upset with Feather for not having warned me about this cultural faux pas.

One night, we bought pastries at a *panadería* and spent the night at a derelict campground. The next morning, I begged Feather to let us return home to my national parks, my safe haven. I did not feel comfortable in my new surroundings: the litter cluttering the roadsides, the street vendors approaching me, the lack of facilities and amenities. I longed for our organized routine of finding a clean, quiet campground, exploring nearby trails, and settling into a safe, restful sleep.

Feather honored my request and we headed back toward the States. I was worried about our 'hippie van' making us a target for questioning at the border. Upon entering Mexico, border officials waved us right through. Returning to the States through customs, however, was more difficult. The customs officers asked us to exit the vehicle and wait inside a room while dogs sniffed around the bus. I sat and waited, my body stiff and on edge. Even though we had nothing to hide, I blinked away tears and had trouble remaining calm.

As Feather and I continued our travels, I grew weary of being on the road, and antsy to develop a plan for what was next. My priority was finding interesting work and settling down for a bit. Even though Feather was ten years older, he had a wandering, free spirit that did not seem keen on settling down any time soon. He had a pilot's license from Alaska and worked at a volunteer fire department. Other than that, I wasn't sure he had any goals or plans for the future. I, on the other hand, had a heart brimming with dreams of my own, and I was worried those might get sidetracked if I stayed with Feather for too long. More than anything, I wanted a career in resource management or environmental education.

"I can't continue living out of a van," I confessed one day.

"It's not forever," Feather said. "What do you want to do instead?"

It wasn't until he'd asked that I knew, very clearly, what I needed to do. "I have to go home."

"Welcome home, sweetie," my mother said once I had returned to the nest. "It is so great to have you back safe and sound."

I was bursting to tell her about all the adventures and hair-raising experiences I'd had. But first, I simply wanted to soak in her unconditional love and support. To get grounded, you go home. After being away for so long, I hadn't realized how much I'd needed to re-ground myself until I was safely home. My mother's love was nurturing and unconditional, which meant that I could return confused and concerned about my path in life, and she would give me the time and space I needed to re-orient.

My whole life, my mother had always encouraged me to follow my dreams and to not worry about settling down and starting a family.

"You may never get married or have kids, and that's okay," my mother reminded me.

At times, it seemed like my mother enjoyed living vicariously through my travels, while still staying rooted at home, committed to work, family, and friends. She seemed happy with the life she had built, and I knew she wanted the same contentment for me.

Being around my strong, independent mother helped me to realize that, despite my strong feelings for Feather, my feelings about my career were stronger. I ached to be on my own and create my own destiny. I worried that Feather's 'drifter' mindset over the long term would cause friction between us, and I knew that he would not soon be ready to settle down. Over several sad phone calls, we ended things, both of us feeling hurt and misunderstood.

Six years later, I saw him in California and we caught up as friends. We reminisced about our road trip, shared stories about our current lives, and parted ways hoping to see each other again—though we never would. It was only long after we had broken up that I identified the real reason I had not wanted to stay with Feather. I had wanted to carve out a life on my own terms, yes. But what I ultimately wanted was to build a life with someone who would want to settle down with me, nurture a long-term partnership, and raise children. Even though my mother had given me permission to follow a path unlike hers, I eventually came to realize that hers was the kind of life I wanted. It would always be important to build adventure and wilderness and a stimulating career into my story, but what I came to realize was that the second half of my story would revolve around building community. I wanted a family. I wanted to follow my heart not just to the most beautiful places in the country, but to the most beautiful people I could find on this planet, and to live out my days in a way that would nurture human connection. I will always be grateful to both Feather and my mother for gently steering me in this direction, and for allowing me to come to this conclusion all on my own.

17
Hundreds of Years of Harvest

As Feather and I drove through Yosemite that first time, I took in the giant sequoias and the sheer white granite monoliths of Half Dome, El Capitan, Washington Column, and Cathedral Peak, and I yearned to learn the story that was told in the geology. I could see how John Muir had been so intrigued by Yosemite's distinct legacy of rock and ice. But, I could also see how this was a place that was more than just its natural history.

Muir wrote that it was a pure, wild place where "no mark of man is visible upon it." In fact, though, the Ahwahnechee people had lived in the place now called Yosemite for at least four thousand years. The Ahwahnechee are comprised of the Miwok, Northern Paiute, Kucadikadi, and Mono Lake tribes.

Ahwahnechee women gathered acorns from black oak trees and used a pounding rock—like a stone pestle—to grind the acorns in mortar holes atop granite boulders on which they sat with friends and family members, telling stories and making the time pass.

Before grinding the acorns, the women would store them in a granary they called a *chuckah*, a large, cylindrical basket woven together by deer brush and tied at the ends with willow stems, then fastened with wild grapevine. The whole thing was supported by incense cedar poles. The chuckah was lined with dry pine needles and wormwood (an effective agent against insects and rodents), then filled with acorns collected in the fall. The harvest was sealed with more pine needles, segments of incense cedar bark, everything bound in place by wild grapevines, then thatched with white fir or more incense cedar to protect against the elements over the winter.

When the women were ready to process the acorns, they would lay them across a slab of rock to dry in the sun. Once dried, the women would sit around cracking and shelling, discarding any undesirable ones, and the acorn kernels were then pounded into a fine yellow meal in the mortar holes atop granite boulders.

They would place the flour in a hard-packed, fern-lined sand basin at the edge of a river and pour warmed spring water over it to remove the bitter tannin. The water would drain into the sand, and this process would be repeated with increasingly warm water until the bitter taste was gone. This leaching process could produce three different end products, depending on the resulting fineness of the meal. The smallest grains were used for a thin soup, the middle consistency for a mush, and the coarse grains for small patties baked on hot, flat rocks. Women cooked the mush in willow baskets that were heated by lowering hot stones onto the mush. Once the mush was cooked through, the stones were removed using long tongs and quickly placed in cold water. The cool temperature of the water made the mush congeal onto the stones, which could then be peeled off for snacking or baked into a flat bread.

Over time, the mortar holes at the tops of the granite boulders deepened and widened from repeated use over centuries. For every inch in depth of the mortars in the rock, researchers estimate one hundred years of grinding acorns, which tells the story of at least eight hundred years of this ritual.

Black oak acorns compromised almost sixty percent of the Ahwahnechee diet. To control the undergrowth and manage the oak population, they would perform controlled burns throughout the valley. These intentional fires would also clear land, open it up by removing detritus and underbrush, make it more usable and easier to travel through, and would also increase the available pastureland for grazing deer. The plants most used by the Ahwahnechee—deer grass for baskets, edible grasses, bulbs, corms, and tubers—were shade-intolerant species that thrived on regular burning, which meant that the fires actually aided in preserving the diverse makeup of the valley's ecosystem. In fact, using tree rings, researchers constructed a map of the valley's forest between the years of 1575 and 2006 to study the impact of controlled burns on biodiversity. The study showed that, due to the decrease of open spaces (historically created from prescribed burns) shade-tolerant trees like white fir and incense cedar populations had increased significantly, now two times more densely packed than in the nineteenth century. After the Native population was removed from Yosemite Valley by the U.S. Army and armed state militia, a century of fire suppression followed. Now, trees are twenty percent smaller, the overall biodiversity in the park has declined, and the forests are so choked and overcrowded that the risk of accidental, large-scale fires has become formidable.

The California Gold Rush of 1849 prompted an influx of thousands of non-Indian miners into the Sierra Nevada to search for gold, after which thousands of Miwok people were either killed or died of starvation. Then, the Mariposa Battalion, a group of state-sponsored vigilantes, snuck into a Native settlement in Yosemite Valley and used embers from the tribe's campfires to burn down wigwams, a tactic borrowed from the Indian Wars known to spark panic and chaos. The fire spread into the forest and dozens of Ahwahnechee fled from their homes. Twenty-three victims were killed and an unreported number of people were wounded. The goal was to relocate the tribes to the Fresno River Reservation, but that attempt and a second one in 1852 were unsuccessful.

As non-Indians began settling in Yosemite, the Native community tried to adapt, swapping their clothing for Euro-American styles and incorporating non-traditional foods into their diets. Native men worked as guides, wood cutters, and wranglers, and the women offered childcare and housekeeping services, along with selling baskets.

By the 1930s, the older Native villages had disbanded. New cabins were built for a modern Native village, but few tribe members could make a living staying in Yosemite. Eventually, the National Park Service dismantled the new village and reconstructed it on the former site of the largest historical Ahwahnechee village, complete with a sweathouse, bark houses, mortar holes, acorn granaries, and a ceremonial roundhouse, which is occasionally used by local tribal members for ceremonies and gatherings.

The longer Muir lived in and studied the ecosystems of Yosemite, the more alarmed he became by the damage livestock animals were causing to the fragile High Sierra. In 1889, he convinced Robert Underwood Johnson, editor of *Century Magazine*, that the only way to save this special place from further destruction would be to incorporate it into a national park. Not long after Johnson published Muir's arguments, a bill was proposed in Congress that led to the designation of Yosemite National Park in 1890.

The fact that Yosemite has been preserved is thanks, in no small part, to Muir's tireless advocacy. But it is also partly due to Muir's purist approach to conservation that the park now poses such an enormous fire risk. Though Muir undoubtedly contributed much to the world of conservation, his stance on wild spaces was clouded by a rigid attitude regarding park management.

The irony is that one of the features of Yosemite that Muir most fell in love with was its ordered beauty, with its 'landscape gardens', giving Yosemite the look of a maintained park. But at the time, it was not yet known that the open meadowlands and clear, well-tended forests were the product of controlled burns by the Native people who had resided in the valley for centuries. Muir was staunchly in support of fire suppression measures, believing that wildfires were a 'master-scourge' against the health of forests, and he advocated for federal protection. However, Yosemite Park officials saw the rationale behind intentional burns and argued that the prevention of fires would lead to 'disastrous results'. Eventually, due to support from prominent politicians and government officials at the time, Muir's case was the victor and before long, the forests became choked with unmitigated growth. Muir had advocated for 'expensive attention' from a 'landscape artist' to maintain the park's orderly appearance, but there were never sufficient funds to pay for such a demanding task. Instead, funds were diverted to now suppressing the unplanned fires that sprang up in the region due to lightning strikes or accidents.

The historic Yellowstone fires of 1988 were a lesson in the devastation that can be caused when fires are provided with heavy fuel loads during hot, dry, windy weather after years of fire suppression. Foresters now understand the beneficial ecological role of fire in forest health and argue that controlled or 'prescribed' burns help tree and plant communities regenerate, keeping fuel loads down and lessening the threat of out-of-control, catastrophic wildfires.

What is interesting is that Muir was certain the only way to keep Yosemite pristine was to prioritize the purity of wilderness above all other concerns, including the displacement of its original inhabitants.

What Muir failed to consider was that the original inhabitants had been the park's stewards for thousands of years, transforming the landscape, but making sure to keep it intact, because Yosemite was their home and in order to continue using its natural resources, they had to take measures to conserve them. This symbiotic order is what has been lacking in global conservation efforts for more than a century. Not considering humans as part of an ecosystem creates conservation-refugees, native inhabitants of a valuable area that are pushed to the edges of it in the name of 'environmental protection'. But what this actually does is limit the number of people who are deeply invested in the conservation of those places.

In 2007, researchers studied the patterns of eighty-four forests in fifteen countries, half of which were nationally protected, and they didn't find any significant differences in vegetation density between protected and unprotected forests. However, one factor stood out. When a forest benefited from the direct involvement of local and indigenous populations who had sovereignty over the management rules, the vegetation densities were considerably higher, regardless of protection status. This points to the possibility that federal protection is not the only—or even superior—way to conserve wild spaces.

Muir's wonderment of the natural world was notable for its valuation of non-human species. What was left lacking was his narrow-minded interpretation of what comprises a whole, healthy ecosystem. There is much to be done within the present-day conservation movement to rectify historical damage. A first step would be to recognize indigenous land rights. It also would seem prudent to empower neighboring communities to take more of a stake in conservation efforts. Finally, it is important that stories of a landscape's history—both human and natural—continue to be shared with visitors.

Within the complex ecosystem of Yosemite, it would be foolhardy to value any species over another, since the web of dependencies is much too complex to try to untangle. The black oaks were not only integral to the survival of human inhabitants in Yosemite, but continue to be a food source for deer, squirrels, black bears, and birds like the acorn woodpecker, which stores acorns inside holes it bores into trees. Cavities in the trunks of mature black oaks offer a home for nesting birds and mammals.

Balancing an ecosystem requires maintaining a balanced environmental ethic—one that doesn't quickly leap to conclusions or certainties, one that allows room for curiosity, and one that holds all species in equal regard.

Yosemite National Park now teems with people. Some find it to be too overrun—a Disneyland of natural wonder. In 2016, over five million sightseers, hikers, campers, and climbers spent time in the park. I am of the mind that the more people who can spend time in nature, the more nature will benefit, as long as visitors respect both the fragile ecosystem and the history. It is the task of every visitor to find what speaks to them and makes them want to invest in the protection of these places. For Muir, it was the glacial geology. For me, it is the grinding sites of the Ahwahnechee.

18
Stronger Together

Unlike gray whales, humpback whales travel in groups. During my time as a naturalist on a sailing vessel in the Gulf of Alaska, I studied humpback whale behavior closely. From the deck of the boat, I witnessed their dazzling cooperative feeding behaviors. Bubble-net feeding is a complex, highly synchronized ritual that involves humpback whales exhaling bubbles in a spiral formation to corral herring, krill, and other food staples into the center. Exhaling the bubbles creates a loud sound that disorients the fish. The whales swim up to the surface, with wide open mouths, which can hold up to fifteen thousand gallons of water. Then, they force water out with their powerful tongues. Humpbacks also perform lateral lunge feeding, where whales swim in pairs and one whale channels the krill and herring into the partner's gaping mouth.

A humpback can eat as much as three thousand pounds of fish a day, snacking around the clock to get their fill. However, they only eat during the summer half of the year, spending the other half focused on breeding. Bubble-net feeding is not instinctual; it is learned. This means that humpback whales have adopted this behavior to feed more mouths at once. In other words, they have learned that teamwork ensures that the whole pod gets enough food.

***

I was lucky enough to spot wolves in the wild on three occasions while living in Denali National Park in Alaska. As I commuted to work from the Toklat River to Wonder Lake, I always trained my eyes on the landscape, looking for patterns of wildlife. One day, to my delight, I saw wolves loping along the tundra with long, easy strides, covering a lot of ground while hunting for squirrels. I even saw a wolf pounce on a squirrel and get his meal. Through research and pleasure reading, I learned about wolf behavior. In *The Wisdom of Wolves: How Wolves Can Teach Us to Be More Human*, wolf expert and naturalist Elli Radinger draws from her twenty-five years of experiences among the wolves of Yellowstone National Park to tell us their remarkable stories. "Wolves aren't wolfish. They can die of broken hearts, show tenderness to their young and elderly, and their packs are led by couples, with the key decisions made by females," Radinger teaches us.

There are approximately fourteen wolf packs in Denali, totaling about a hundred animals. When they are two to three years old, wolves begin pairing off and mating, sometimes establishing lifelong partners. They raise their pups in dens, often returning to the same den each year. The wolf pups are collectively cared for by the entire pack, weaning off their mother's milk after the first month, then relying on a diet of regurgitated meat from other pack members. At one or two years old, a young wolf can leave the pack to find a mate and form its own pack, some of these lone wolves traveling as far as five hundred miles to find their new home.

***

In the subalpine zone on the south side of the Alaska Range mountains in Denali National Park, the landscape is always shifting, adjusting from disturbances like rockslides and avalanches, settling and rebalancing. Alder trees prefer steep terrain and disturbed mineral soil, so the south side of the range offers optimal conditions for alders to grow and spread into impenetrable thickets. Not only do alders help to stabilize the landscape, but the nodules of their roots provide a home for the bacterium Frankia to grow, along with sugars from their photosynthetic process. Frankia, in turn, assists alders in their growth, fixing nitrogen in the atmosphere, and making it available as a nutrient source to the roots of the alders.

These organisms benefit from cooperative behavior, living in sustained harmony. I am always looking for relationships and patterns like this in nature, learning what I can from these organisms that have somehow discovered mutually beneficial ways of living and thriving in harsh environments.

***

When I worked at Shasta-Trinity National Forest as a climbing ranger, I partnered with an extraordinary alpinist who taught me to trust my instincts, my climbing partner, the rope, and the process. He had great faith in his skills and never seemed to entertain the luxury of a negative thought. When we climbed routes on Mount Shasta, I dug my ice ax in hard while I had him on belay to hold his unlikely slip and I knew he would never let me take a hard fall. I appreciated that he treated me as an equal while fully knowing that he had more and varied skills. He was a confident and competent climber and partnering with him helped build my confidence and skill set as well. Most of all, I loved being around his positive optimism and outlook on life.

Most days on the clock, I had the task of trudging up the regular route on Mount Shasta, feeling safe and secure, going about my job responsibilities, checking for permits, ensuring that minimum camping techniques were being adhered to, and performing search and rescue operations when needed. When time permitted, my partner was always keen on exploring a more remote and unclimbed section of the mountain. Together, we achieved what one could not on our own. That is the beauty of having a climbing partner that you rely on and trust. Our interdependence was serving as a stunning testament to the cooperative power of two humans joining together to succeed in a shared goal. I would carry this lesson with me to the summits of Kilimanjaro, Mount Rainier, and Gokyo Ri in Nepal, each with trustworthy, supportive partners.

19
Women of the World

A main struggle of my life has been to strike the right balance between independence and community, adventure and home. It has helped to know powerful, competent, caring, beautiful women who have given me myriad examples for how to navigate this predicament that is particular to women: that tension between caregiving and taking time for ourselves. As women in a patriarchal society, we have been conditioned to serve others before we serve ourselves. Even with a dozen children, I saw that my mother was able to strike that balance between motherhood and work. My four gorgeous sisters were, for me, a lesson in what happens when women always have one another's backs, through thick and thin, and how the security of that stronghold can make it feel safe enough to venture into the world alone. I have also known women who have shown me that it is possible to live without a partner or children and to feel just as fulfilled in this one life.

When I worked in Yosemite, I taught Elderhostel groups (now called Road Scholar), which offered experimental learning opportunities for adults. During one such course, I was fortunate enough to meet Joan, with whom I immediately connected. She had a zest for life and a warm, welcoming demeanor. When I told her I wanted to study in an intensive summer dance program in Colorado, Joan invited me to come stay with her in Boulder. I took her up on the offer and she became my 'mom of the West'. My biological mother even came and stayed with her a few times and it was a joy to have both of my 'moms' together.

In Joan's basement there was a huge map of the world on the wall, dotted with at least three hundred pins that marked the places she had traveled around the globe.

When Joan joined a safari in Africa, the Jeep driver hit a large pothole so hard that Joan broke her tailbone. Being the trooper she was, she continued on with the safari, managing her own pain, camera in hand and donut pillow under her backside. Her photo collection of all her trips taken over the course of a lifetime—more than sixty years—is encyclopedic. In the time we spent together, she told me all about her travels, her Semesters at Sea, her treks all over Asia, and her many Elderhostel trips.

One time, several years later, I ran into Joan in the Alaska bush. "Joan, is that you?" I asked in disbelief. "What are you doing in Alaska?"

"Fancy meeting you here," she said. "I'm on another Elderhostel trip."

We hugged, shared stories from our experiences in Alaska, and she headed off to dinner with her cohort group.

I often teased Joan about the potential for finding love or partnership through the Elderhostel program. "You know, Joan," I'd remind her, "there have been many matches made during these trips. People end up together or make a habit of going on trips together."

But, much like my own mother, Joan was an independent soul who clearly did not need a man in her life—or at least didn't feel compelled to seek one out. Though, unlike my stay-close-to-home mother, Joan had nary a worry about setting out on her own travels or on one of these guided trips. Joan was content to find community wherever she went, running into people like me in the far north, making connections that would last the rest of her life, even if they weren't romantic ones.

No matter what types of women I meet, I continue to be amazed at the range of lives women can lead, taking lessons from each person along the way. I have female friends who have worked with children as teachers and mentors, giving more of their time and energy than most people I know. I have a friend who has been a flight attendant for nearly thirty years, successfully making travel not only a lifestyle, but a job. I know women who have worked with troubled teens in Northern California among the Redwoods. I have many healing friends who are bodyworkers, massage, or physical therapists. I have colleagues from my time in an undergraduate program who are still working in the environmental field. Many from my graduate program are in the counseling or helping professions. All these women have nurtured their own families and other people's families, cared for their neighbors and communities, tended and protected the Earth, and still made time for meaningful friendships along the way. But maybe most importantly, they have all made sure that they are following paths they have chosen, rather than lives that have been imposed on them by society, family, or work. It is not an easy path—to nurture oneself—but it must take priority for all the rest to fall into place.

20
Belonging

Growing up, our house was always brimming with activity. It was busy and boisterous. But my most vivid memories are from what happened outside our house, when we spent time in our family's rustic log cabin in Adirondack Park in northern New York each summer. We would spend two weeks swimming in freshwater lakes, picking tart wild blueberries, lounging in the sunshine, and getting sunburned.

I recall smoky bonfires that glowed against the night sky, crackling and shooting red-hot glowing embers our way. My brothers went fishing and brought home perch, bullhead, and the occasional trout. I never cared for seeing the fish guts, so I would disappear while they cleaned them, then strategically reappear right as the boys were grilling them over the open fire.

Out there, the older siblings would get driving lessons. During the day drives, we would roll down the car windows and sit on the window frame, throwing stones at trees and signs for target practice. I loved the feeling of fresh air blowing through my long brown hair in the mountains and smelling the scent of pine in the breeze. The highlight was driving down dirt roads looking for wildlife in the evening's fading light. At night, the drives were stealthier, and we often saw deer jumping across the road, rabbits scurrying around, and, if we were lucky, a black bear appearing at the edge of the woods.

Back at home, on Sundays, my father made sure it was 'family day', which meant that no neighbor kids were allowed in the yard to play, nor could we head over to friends' houses. My father recognized the importance of building a close-knit community within our own family, and he made sure that was prioritized so that we could feel the strength of our bonds. His legacy held us together like glue. After he died, my siblings and I banded together to support one another as we raised a village. Even amid the frenetic energy of such a full house, life ran smoothly. We worked as a team, helping my mother where we could. My older siblings who had learned how to drive on those backroads chauffeured the younger kids around. Even when some of us left home, we always returned, always bound to the place that that nurtured our roots and instilled in us a lasting sense of belonging. In the end, that is what community is all about—whether people are blood-related or tied together by common interests, community offers an individual the sense that they fit within a greater whole.

Afterword

When people ask which national park is my favorite, I often respond that it is whichever park I am currently exploring and enjoying. While every park I have worked in will always hold special places in my heart, I try not to let myself get too stuck in the past. Nostalgia and fond memories, if left unchecked, can have a way of robbing joy and gratitude from the present moment. If I let myself become too wistful about past loves or carefree summers awash in sunshine, I might find it harder to appreciate the life I am currently living, with my dear husband and amazing children, in a place that I now call home. Whenever I visit national parks, I do my best to remain present and engaged, staying curious about the native flora and fauna, about the particular personality of the place, about the human history, and about the complex land management and conservation issues that are playing out in these wild spaces. I try to actively practice gratitude for the park's founders and the forethought that made these parks accessible to people like me, while also honoring the people and other organisms who first called these places home.

Some visitors drive to a park, stop at the gift shop, and take a few photos from the car. As for fully appreciating a park, I am inclined to agree with Edward Abbey's words in *Desert Solitaire*, who said something like: "You can't see anything from a car; you've got to get out of the darn contraption and walk, better yet crawl, on hands and knees, over the sandstone and through the thornbush and cactus."

I do agree that the outdoors should not just be *seen*, but *experienced*. Pay the fee. Start walking. I guarantee that as soon as you get at least five minutes away from the car, something will happen. You might spot a chipmunk munching on a snack, or a lizard doing pushups on a warm rock. If you are quiet, you might hear a bird call or see a family of deer. Preferably, get as far away from any road as you can. Be prepared and leave no trace. Don't litter. Go with friends. Store food properly so you don't get cited by a ranger. Don't feed the animals. Open your eyes.

These days, you can find amazing videos on the internet that can provide a sense of escapism to the wilderness. YouTube allows people to see nature from the comfort of their couches. A perfect example of such a 'channel' is Alexander Ayling's documentaries of his adventures (a favorite is his Milford Track documentary). Ayling narrates as he goes and adds inspirational messages. "What do we learn on an adventure like this? Perhaps we don't learn anything that we didn't already know—we are just reminded of this ancient knowledge that lives deep within all of us. The knowledge that we are a part of this world, not apart from it. That we are as at home in the forests, mountains and streams as we are in our apartments, condos, and houses. That we need to protect the wild places that remain, if only to remind us of who we are in an age where so few of us remember to reconnect with the ancient identities within, our ancestors of the alpine, forebears of the forest, mothers of the mountains, and relatives of the rivers. We journey into the wild to find the person who lives within us all, the children of the forest and the sun."

It is wonderful to see that these places are captured in a way that allows people who are not capable of doing these kinds of treks to appreciate places they might otherwise never get to experience. The followers get to enjoy the hikes vicariously through the filmmaker. People fall more in love with nature when they can see it and are more motivated to want to protect and preserve these wild places.

***

I enjoy using products that bring the outdoors into my home, onto my body, and into my surroundings. I especially love products by ISUN Skincare, a wild-crafted skincare line that infuses the Colorado mountain wilderness into their lotions, oils, and creams. Bunnie, the owner, is an excellent role model for women who want to find their purpose and achieve their goals through a combination of grit and environmental ethics. She is an example of how, if you follow your passion, the rest will follow. On her ranch, Bunnie uses spring water and home-grown plants for her products.

Yet, despite how exciting outdoor adventure YouTube videos can be or how nourishing Bunnie's glorious, earthy products feel on your skin, there will never be a substitute for dipping your bare feet into the cold rush of river water. You will not get to smell the sage or creosote in the desert, or the brine and salty fresh air of the ocean. You will not get to bend over and sink your hand into a spongy mass of moss at the base of an ancient, giant Sitka spruce. So, for those who are able, I hope you take the time to plan your next trip and get out into the environment in the ways you most enjoy.

***

I think about surfers and how they ride the crests of waves, and what that process looks like. Maneuvering a surfboard is something completely foreign to this landlocked mountain girl, but when I visit the ocean, I like to observe the way the surfers sit, how they feel the ebb and flow of the ocean beneath their boards. I sense their anticipation as they wait for the perfect wave. They watch for incoming waves, measuring their volume, energy, and potential. Then, in a split second, they make their move and paddle hard toward shore to gain momentum. Then, if the wave catches their board just right, they hop up and feel the pull of the ocean beneath their feet, sending them flying across saltwater, carrying them along.

The hanging out part looks peaceful and serene. I can imagine floating out there with the other surfers, letting the rhythmic cadence of the waves lull me into a trance. The rest of the sport looks a bit terrifying. Water is a powerful thing, and the force behind a large wave can send a person tumbling through a churning mess of froth that can leave them disoriented and shaken. Under the water, they might not know which way is up or down. They might begin to panic about when they can take their next breath. But I have spoken with surfers, and they all agree that the risks are worth the rewards. To feel one with the water, to enjoy the thrill of speed and synchronicity—this joy is unmatched.

Finding joy in wilderness is not exclusive to thrill seekers. Quieter activities like fly fishing achieve the same level of pleasure. The fly fisherwoman patiently waits for the rise of a trout from the surface of the water. When she finally lands a 'lunker', her heart seizes onto the same kind of joy as the surfer. She carefully unhooks the fish from her line, photographs its brilliant colors glinting in sunshine, then releases it back into the water, grateful for the quiet thrill, and ready to cast again.

In the end, I believe it is better to challenge ourselves than to sit back and be lulled into complacence or too much comfort. Let's get uncomfortable. Let's get dirt under our fingernails and get bitten by mosquitoes and see our breath in the biting cold. Let's choose the role models who push us out of our comfort zones, so that we might realize our true potential. I have my own role models across all arenas—artists, authors, actors, adventurers—and they have all helped to shape me into the person I most want to be. In Jen Sincero's *You Are a Badass: How to Stop Doubting Your Greatness and Start Living an Awesome Life*, she writes:

"Appreciate how special you are. There will never be anyone exactly like you. You were given special gifts and talents to share with the world, and even though everybody has special gifts and talents, nobody will use theirs in quite the same way you do. You have a way of being in the world and a perspective that's unique to you. You are the only one who thinks your thoughts the way you think them. You have created your own unique reality and are living your life according to your own unique path. You are the only one you that will ever be. You are kind of a big deal."

I will always keep this book and reread it again and again. Her advice seeps into my conscious and unconscious mind. Sincero pushes us to take action and to jump off the cliff, to take the risk, to believe in ourselves, and to know that we are badasses in every way. (Of course, I had to read this book because my initials, B.A., earned me the nickname 'Badass'). Sincero's words have helped to reassure me that I was always on the right path, and her book has encouraged and propelled me further.

My hope is that my little book helps people of all ages know that they can go out and have adventures, mishaps and losses, then go right back out and have more adventures, mishaps, and losses. If they are truly choosing self-love and following their joy, then they will survive and thrive—just like badasses do.

In the simplest of terms, just listen to and be yourself. We are the authors of our own journey. I hope you are inspired to go out and get out after it! Happy trails and many blessings to all.

Selected Reading

Abbey, Edward, *Desert Solitaire: A Season in the Wilderness* (New York: Ballantine Books, 1968).

Anderson, M. Kat, and Michael J. Moratto, *Native American Land-Use Practices and Ecological Impacts*, USGS II, Chapter 9, https://pubs.usgs.gov/dds/dds-43/VOL_II/VII_C09.PDF.

Duckworth, A. L., et al., "Cognitive and noncognitive predictors of success," Proceedings of the National Academy of Sciences, (2019), 116(47), https://doi.org/10.1073/pnas.1910510116.

Galton, Francis, Hereditary Genius: An Inquiry Into Its Laws and Consequences (Macmillan and Co., 1869).

"Indigenous Plants and Native Uses in the Northeast," NativeTech: Native American Technology and Art.

http://www.nativetech.org/plantgath/cattail.htm.

Johnson, Eric Michael, "How John Muir's Brand of Conservation Led to the Decline of Yosemite," *Scientific American*, August 13, 2014, https://blogs.scientificamerican.com/primate-diaries/how-john-muir-s-brand-of-conservation-led-to-the-decline-of-yosemite/

Kennedy, Michael, Access and the Politics of Climbing: A Long Simmering Stew, 41 Am. Alpine. J. 73 (1999).

Ketcham, Christopher, "The End of the (Green) River," Men's Journal, https://www.mensjournal.com/travel/the-end-of-the-green-river-20130807/.

"Marjory Stoneman Douglas," Everglades, NPS.gov, last modified June 20, 2020, https://www.nps.gov/ever/learn/historyculture/stoneman-douglas.htm.

Meine, Curt, *Aldo Leopold: His Life and Work* (Madison, Wis.: University of Wisconsin Press, 1988).

Muir, John, "My First Summer in the Sierra (Part IV)," *The Atlantic*, April, 1911, https://www.theatlantic.com/magazine/archive/1911/04/my-first-summer-in-the-sierra-part-iv/543663/.

Nijhuis, Michelle, "Don't Cancel John Muir," *The Atlantic*, April 12, 2021, https://www.theatlantic.com/ideas/archive/2021/04/conservation-movements-complicated-history/618556/.

"Plants," Crater Lake, NPS.gov, last modified May 3, 2022, https://www.nps.gov/crla/learn/nature/plants.htm.

"Plants," Everglades, NPS.gov, last modified March 12, 2021, https://www.nps.gov/ever/learn/nature/plants.htm.

"Plants," Grand Canyon, NPS.gov, last modified October 21, 2021, https://www.nps.gov/grca/learn/nature/plants.htm.

Radinger, Elli H., The Wisdom of Wolves: How Wolves Can Teach Us to Be More Human (Michael Joseph, 2022).

Sammartino, Michael, "To Bolt or Not to Bolt: A Framework for Common Sense Climbing Regulation," American Bar Association, August 24, 2020, https://www.americanbar.org/groups/environment_energy_resources/publications/plr/20200824-to-bolt-or-not-to-bolt/.

Schaffer, Jeffrey P, "The Living Yosemite: The Ahwahnechee," 100 Yosemite Hikes.

Sierra, Janet L., "Cattails and Native American Culture," Institute for American Indian Studies Medicinal Monday, February 19, 2018, https://patch.com/connecticut/woodbury-middlebury/cattails-native-american-culture

Sincero, Jen, You Are a Badass: How to Stop Doubting Your Greatness and Start Living an Awesome Life

(Philadelphia: Running Press Adult, 2013), 55.

Sugihara, Neil G., et al., *Fire in California's Ecosystems* (Berkeley: University of California Press, 2006), 418.

"Their Lifeways," Yosemite, National Parks Service, last modified November 17, 2018, https://www.nps.gov/yose/learn/historyculture/their-lifeways.htm

"The Yosemite Indians . . . And How They Lived Their Lives," Undiscovered-Yosemite.com, http://www.undiscovered-yosemite.com/yosemite-indians.html

Wilson, Herbert Earl. The Lore and Lure of Yosemite. n.d.

"Zion's Natural Diversity," Plants / Animals, ZionNationalPark.com, https://zionnationalpark.com/explore/guidebook/plants-animals/#:~:text=Plants%20vary%2C%20as%20fir%2C%20ponderosa,found%20in%20Zion%20National%20Park.

Acknowledgments

Thank you to all of my beta readers, editors, and friends who helped me along the way, including Heather Hansen, author of *Wildfire: On the Front Lines with Station 8* and *Prophets and Moguls, Rangers and Rogues, Bison and Bears: 100 Years of the National Park Service*; Randi Minetor of Lyons Press, who wrote the series of books detailing misadventures in our national parks, among many other Falcon Guide books and a special book called *Backyard Birding*; and the author of *Point of Direction*, Rachel Weaver, who inspired me with her descriptive writing and kind and caring heart. Also, to fellow Ranger Andrea Lankford who wrote *Ranger Confidential: Living, Working, and Dying in the National Parks*, thank you for your camaraderie.

Early influencers were Pam Houston of *Cowboys Are My Weakness* fame, and *Deep Creek*, and of course, Cheryl Strayed of *Wild* and Elizabeth Gilbert with her highly praised *Eat, Pray, Love*; *Committed;* *Big Magic*; and *City of Girls*.

More recent interests include deep thought-inducing painter Rachel Pohl and conservationist

Charles Post, who is a fellow at The Explorer's Club, as well as my friend director/producer Ben Masters of the films *Unbranded* and *The River and The Wall*. Many happy returns to you all. Thank you for all of your good work.

This collection of stories would not be complete without giving a shoutout to some of the greatest teachers, guides, rangers, and outdoor educators that work in our classrooms, parks, and wildlands who educate future generations about the importance of conservation, preservation, and the continuance of caring for the natural world. Organizations like NatureBridge, Outward Bound, Trek Travel and National Outdoor Leadership School are often seeking out qualified candidates to help guide their trips of a lifetime.

About the Author

B.A. Woodland was born in Central New York and traveled out West as a young woman to forge her own path in the wild, open expanses of some of America's most prized and protected public lands. Dear to her heart were experiences as a National Park Service ranger in Grand Canyon, Crater Lake, Zion, Yosemite, Mount Rainier, and Denali National Parks. From working as a canoe guide in the Everglades of Florida to scaling a Cascade volcano as a climbing ranger on Mount Shasta in California, B.A. likes to explore new environments and test her mettle while learning and educating others about the marvels of the natural world. Being comfortable with taking risks and trusting others took time for the daughter who lost her father at the age of six. True to the story is the question: How does one overcome the loss of a parent at a young age? What comes as somewhat of a surprise is her determination to build trust in herself and others, cultivate community wherever she landed, and strive to deepen loving relationships. Hers is a story of hope, the healing power of nature, and love.